THE BUSY
COOK'S BOOK

THE BUSY
COOK'S BOOK

Pamela Westland

CONTENTS

First published in 1983 by Octopus Books Limited
59 Grosvenor Street, London W1

Sixth impression, 1985

© 1983 Hennerwood Publications Limited

ISBN 0 86273 068 6

Produced by Mandarin
Publishers Ltd
22a Westlands Road
Quarry Bay
Hong Kong

Printed in Hong Kong

INTRODUCTION

Preparing and cooking a meal for family and friends is an exciting challenge – and one which this book helps you to meet successfully, over and over again. Whether you are looking for speedy new ideas for family snacks; need inspiration when you have only minutes between dashing home and serving a meal, or want something simple yet impressive to offer your guests – read on!

The title has been taken literally. Busy cooks don't have time to wade through pages of text, and so the recipes are set out in the most helpful way possible. At a glance, you can choose the chapter to suit the occasion – whether you have 15, 30, 45 minutes or 1 hour to cook, want to prepare one dish or a complete meal in advance, or want a balanced menu worked out for you.

Check on your kitchen equipment, take good care of non-stick surfaces, keep appliances in good working order, and make sure that everything is close at hand. Just moving your most frequently used gadgets from one drawer to another nearer the sink or cooker; making space for the mixer to be at the ready on the work top, and adding a few inexpensive tools to your armoury could be the key to hours of extra leisure time over the years.

Kitchen Equipment

Knives Choose the best you can afford and keep them sharp. (Non-stainless steel knives keep sharper for longer.) You need straight-edged blades for chopping, dicing and shredding and scallop- or serrated-edged ones for the 'sawing' motion jobs – slicing bread, meat, frozen foods and fruit, especially those with obstinate skins, like tomatoes. Keep to stainless steel knives for cutting acidic ingredients, such as lemons.

Hand tools Time-savers include: good-quality kitchen scissors for snipping everything from bacon rinds to chives; an apple corer, which cuts decorative butter pats and carrot slices, too; mandoline slicer to cut wafer-thin slices of vegetables that then cook in a trice, and to slice quickly through cucumber; fruit zester, to scrape rapidly across lemon and orange rind; one-handed whisk, to leave the other hand free for pouring; a stiff vegetable brush, to brush along the grain to clean celery and to scrub root vegetables, and a salad spinner to make short work of drying lettuce, watercress and all blanched vegetables and fruit before freezing.

Weights and measures Weighing scales with a re-zero dial are quick and easier to calculate as you add one ingredient to another in the bowl; a jug or bowl with a millilitre fluid ounce scale is helpful when measuring liquids, and a set of spoons in the standard measures (see below) can often save weighing at all.

Utensils Flameproof casseroles save time and washing up. You can pre-fry vegetables and meat, continue cooking on the hotplate or in the oven, and take the dish straight to the table. One-pot cooking was invented for the busy cook! Non-stick pans and bakeware of all kinds save most pre-greasing, make flipping, tossing and turning easier – and avoid breaking the food in the process. Again, buy the best you can afford. This is where quality really counts.

Electrical equipment

Liquidizers, crumb bread and biscuits, grate nuts and cheese, make fruit and vegetable purée (soups in seconds!), mix batters and sauces, make creamy pâté, and foolproof mayonnaise.

Electric mixers, with the various attachments, whip, whisk, cream, beat, chop, slice, shred, mince, grind and sieve.

Food processors, with an assortment of discs, cope with every preparation stage except whipping cream and sieving.

Contact grills, table-top cooking at double-quick speed. They can grill, bake, fry, braise, boil, roast and toast. Everything from pastry to pâté cooks speedily to perfection.

Sandwich makers, sealed-in sandwiches, pastries, bread rolls, cakes, scones – the appliances are much more versatile than they seem.

Slow-cookers, cook casseroles, puddings, pâtés, soups, vegetables slowly and surely – the perfect away-day method of cooking at a controlled temperature.

Pressure cookers, the original fast-cookers, especially time-saving for cheaper cuts of meat, root vegetables, dried pulses, steamed puddings. The longer ingredients take to cook by conventional means, the greater the time saving.

Steamers and rice cookers, cook rice to perfection and keep it hot, and steam meat, fish, fruit and vegetables, on an open rack or tastily sealed in foil parcels.

Good stand-buys

It's reassuring to keep a small and carefully chosen stock of the canned, packaged and frozen foods you find most versatile. Here are some reminders.

Canned goods

Peeled tomatoes are time-savers for sauces, soup, casseroles. Consommé makes a good instant soup with a dash of sherry and a tastier beef stock than bouillon cubes. The condensed kind doubles for 'meat glaze' and, when chilled, can be chopped and mixed with cold meats, even melon, as a salad. Tuna fish turns green salad into a French-style meal, makes a marvellous sauce for pasta or rice and a filling for pastry cases. All canned fruits are useful, some are more versatile than others. Grapefruit segments mixed with sliced avocado, or grilled with brandy butter make a stunning first course. Peach or apricot halves grilled or stuffed and baked soon cast off the 'canned' label.

Dry goods Check stocks regularly, or keep them in glass jars so you can see when the level's dropped. Ring the changes with brown and white rice, wholemeal and refined ('ordinary') pasta in all shapes and sizes. Have a colourful selection of dried pulses – orange and brown lentils, red kidney beans, green mung beans, white haricots and cut down on cooking time – usually by at least half – by pressure cooking them.

Frozen foods Make a selection of vegetables to give variety of shape and colour when your main dish **needs it – broccoli, peas, carrots, sweetcorn, green** beans, spinach – and have some quick-cook chips for those who insist! Choose quick-thawing fruits like raspberries, blackcurrants and bilberries and when you have time, make fruit purée for quick and delicious sauces. Ice cream, home-made or bought, ensures you are never without a dessert, and the new cubes of frozen cream make sure you always have something to top it with. Keep a stock of bought shortcrust and puff pastry, and have some ready-baked pastry cases in all shapes and sizes – tartlets, flan cases, vol-au-vents and even cheese straws. They're great sometimes instead of bread. Have bread rolls (quicker to thaw than a loaf) and, if you make your own, freeze some bread dough for on-the-spot baking. Be meticulous about freezing soups, sauces, pâté, dips in the handy sizes you use – it's easier to use two packs than to cut one in half!

Hints At various points in the book there are boxed hints to give you extra information on such things as cooking methods, marinades and food preparation.

Handy spoon measures

All spoon measures in this book are level. Here are some useful weight equivalents.

10 tablespoons	=150 ml (¼ pt)
1 tablespoon flour	=15 g (½ oz)
1 tablespoon cornflour	=15 g (½ oz)
1 tablespoon breadcrumbs	=10 g (¼ oz)
1 tablespoon ground almonds	=15 g (½ oz)
1 tablespoon whole blanched almonds	=15 g (½ oz)
2 tablespoons rice	=35 g (1¼ oz)
2 tablespoons sugar	=35 g (1¼ oz)
2 tablespoons desiccated coconut	=15 g (½ oz)
2 teaspoons powdered gelatine	=10 g (¼ oz)

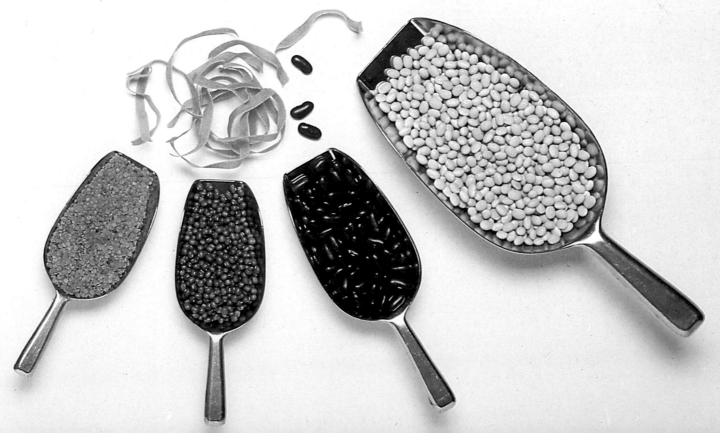

Thinking ahead

Use any little time you have to spare to save extra-precious moments when you're busy.
* A day or two in advance, chop herbs for garnishes, slice or chop mushrooms, onions, carrots (but never vegetables like parsnips, which discolour) and store them in covered containers in the refrigerator.
* Segment or slice oranges and grapefruit, squeeze orange or lemon juice and grate the rind – citrus fruits can be prepared 2 or 3 days in advance.
* Seed grapes (or use seedless ones!) and stone cherries up to 2 days in advance.
* Make syrup for fruit salad – try flavouring it by infusing a bay leaf or twist of orange peel – and keep it in the refrigerator for up to 4 days.
* Use washed yogurt pots, margarine tubs and cream cartons, all with lids, for storing these advance preparations. But remember to label them clearly. A frantic last-minute search for a spoonful of parsley saves neither time nor temper!
* Make shortbread, flapjacks and honey biscuits that keep well in a tin. When you have a 'bought' pudding, it's nice to serve something home-made with it.
* Chop, flake, grate or grind nuts. Toast nuts when you're using the oven or grill. They all store for several weeks in a screw-top jar.
* Make the roux – the butter and flour paste – for sweet and savoury white sauces and store it for up to a week in a covered container in the refrigerator. When it is time to make the sauce, heat the roux gently in a pan, then gradually pour on hot milk or other liquid.
* Practise batch cooking for the refrigerator or freezer to save time, fuel and washing up.

Beating the clock

* When spooning or weighing honey or syrup, flour the spoon or scales first – it rolls off like a dream!
* You know about dipping peaches, apples and tomatoes into boiling water for a few seconds before peeling them. Try the same trick for citrus fruits.
* Never waste anything. Especially an opportunity to cook ahead. When you've boned a joint to stuff it, or filleted fish, use the bones with chopped onion, carrots, celery and herbs to make a basic meat or fish stock. Freeze and store it for up to 3 months.
* When you have some wine left over from one dish – or from a meal – use it to prepare another. Poach apples or pears in red wine spiced with cinnamon or cloves; use wine instead of water for the syrup for extra-special fruit salads. Or freeze the wine in cubes.

In 15 minutes

Rushing in from work or the shops; with unexpected guests 'just called in', but looking hungry, what can you cook in fifteen minutes? Lots of things, from simple snacks like pan-fried egg and bacon and cheese-topped apple rings, to really super main dishes that are fit for a supper party. You will enjoy trying prawns in garlic butter, or pan-fried steak criss-crossed with anchovies.

When time is so precious, it's best to spend it all on the main dish and keep the accompaniments to the minimum. Rice and pasta – no scraping, peeling or chopping – come to the rescue again and again.

And for desserts? Even as the minutes tick away, there's time for baked, grilled or fried fruit, chilled creamy concoctions with fruit and nuts or a toffee-coloured high-rise omelette. All in 15 minutes or less!

In 30 minutes

After cooking a main dish in a quarter of an hour, 30 minutes seems quite a luxury! Using quickly-cooked cuts of meat like pork tenderloin, lamb chops, bacon steaks and liver, or fillets of fish, you can produce really tempting meals. The secret is in the simple-but-good sauces – orange and ginger, pimento mayonnaise and cucumber sauce for example – and the little 'extras' that make all the difference, herbs, spices and flavoured butters for cooking and glazing.

Foil-wrapping food – we suggest plaice and mushrooms in sweet and sour sauce – saves all the last-minute flurry of serving and all the tell-tale smells that can waft from the kitchen.

Fresh fruit is a positive boon when time is at a premium – here, in the recipes for Peach Caramels and Poached Pears with Chocolate Sauce, are two more ideas for a glamorous presentation to lift it into the realms of party fare.

In 45 minutes

In this amount of time, there's more opportunity to use the oven, to prepare fresh vegetables and to make lovely warm and welcoming puddings. Mix and match these ideas and you find you can easily prepare two courses well within your deadline. While thin, tender strips of beef are cooking in red wine, you could make Date and Syrup Pancakes. And with Blue Cheese Pudding in the oven, Peaches in Marmalade Sauce could be sizzling to spicy perfection on a lower shelf.

A few extra minutes spent in preparing a dish can more than pay dividends when it comes to cooking. Cut vegetables into florets or slices, meat into matchstick strips or a joint of lamb into rolled cutlets and the cooking time is minimized.

In an hour

An hour to produce the main dish or a complete meal gives you a little breathing space. It gives you time to prepare the dish and set it to cook, then go away and lay the table, put away the shopping or see to all the other things that are crying out for attention around the house. For whoever enjoys the luxury of a whole hour without interruptions?

The recipes in this chapter make allowance for that, and certainly do not claim your undivided attention.

While the sweet and sour lamb is becoming more tender by the minute, you have time to make a batch of pancakes. While the brown rice is simmering to a delicious nutty tenderness and the vegetables are steaming, there's plenty of time to whip up a pudding from one of the earlier chapters. And while a tangy, filling lemon pudding is steaming away, you could be turning your attention to one of the quickie-cooked grilled or pan-fried dishes. And still have precious moments to spare!

Ahead of time

Some of the dishes in this chapter, such as the Soused Herrings and Coriander Lamb, can be made more than a day ahead. As with all spiced dishes, advance cooking is a positive advantage for it allows the flavours to blend and mellow. Another plus point: meat actually tenderizes as it spends this extra time marinating in its sauce.

Cooking ahead of time definitely does not imply that you have all the time in the world – though there might be the infrequent occasion when you want to spend a little longer on the preparation. And so some dishes in this section, Potted Bacon and Blue Cheese Mousse, Ginger Biscuit Cream Cake and Orange and Nut Pashka, are so snappy, they could be in the first two chapters.

When moments count, don't stop at cooking and preparing the food ahead of time. Do everything you can to set the table in advance, or at least sort out the china and cutlery. Assemble any jars – chutneys or pickles – that might have found their way to the back of the cupboards. Check the cruets, make the mustard, arrange the flowers. No matter how little you find to do in advance, that little will be an enormous help on the day. And just knowing that it is done, another thing ready and waiting, gives your confidence a boost. And that's what *enjoying* serving a meal to family and friends is all about!

Menus

Even when you are entertaining friends to lunch or supper, it isn't always possible to spend as much time as you would like, preparing and cooking the meal.

Our menus make allowance for this, and help you to plan each meal with at least one course prepared in advance, reassuringly ready to serve or just to assemble at the meal-time. In many cases this at-the-ready dish is the first course – Potato and Mortadella Salad, Smoked Mackerel and Cream Cheese Pâté or Pears with Camembert Sauce are examples. And many of these 'starter' suggestions have other possibilities, too. With another salad and a basket of hot, crusty bread rolls or a French loaf they make a perfect light lunch or supper dish.

In all menu planning balance is the key word – balance of the nutritional values of the ingredients, of the colours, textures, flavours and – not least – the cost. That is why fruit and vegetables feature strongly in many of our menus – they come out tops in all these ways.

Whether you plan an up-to-the-minute high-fibre meal (Menu 2), a low-cost family supper (Menu 3) or a special dinner for your guests (Menu 7), the same principles apply. This careful selection of dishes allows you more time to relax with your family and friends, and requires the minimum of last-minute attention in the kitchen.

IN FIFTEEN MINUTES

POACHED TROUT

4 medium rainbow trout, cleaned
150 ml (¼ pint) dry cider (or use lemonade)
a few parsley stalks
1 medium onion, peeled and sliced
2 slices of lemon
6 black peppercorns
150 ml (¼ pint) double cream
salt
freshly ground black pepper
sprigs of parsley, to garnish

Preparation and cooking time: 15 minutes

1. Simmer the trout, in a covered pan, in the cider with the parsley stalks, onion, lemon and peppercorns for 10-12 minutes, until the fish are just cooked.
2. Strain the liquor into a small pan and bring it rapidly to the boil. Immediately lower the heat, stir in the cream and just heat through. Remove from the heat and season the sauce with salt and pepper.
3. Pour the sauce over the fish and garnish with the parsley sprigs.
4. Very small new potatoes may be cooked in the same time, and are a perfect accompaniment.

SMOKED MACKEREL AND ORANGE KEBABS

1 × 175 g (6 oz) packet par-cooked long-grain rice
salt
15 g (½ oz) butter
juice and rind of ½ orange
4 medium fillets of smoked mackerel, skinned
1 teaspoon lemon juice
freshly ground black pepper
3 large oranges, peeled and segmented
2 tablespoons blanched almonds
1 bunch watercress, trimmed, to garnish

Preparation and cooking time: 15 minutes

1. Cook the rice in boiling, salted water for 10 minutes, or until it is just tender. Drain the rice and stir in the butter, orange juice and orange rind. Keep the rice warm.
2. While the rice is cooking, cut the mackerel fillets across into 2.5 cm (1 inch) strips and toss them in the lemon juice. Sprinkle with pepper. Thread the mackerel strips and orange segments alternately on to 4 skewers. Grill under a preheated hot grill for 5 minutes, turning the skewers once.
3. Scatter the almonds on a clean baking sheet and toast them for 2 minutes, turning them once.
4. Just before serving, stir the toasted almonds into the rice. Serve the skewers on the rice and garnish the dish with the watercress sprigs.

PRAWNS IN GARLIC BUTTER

1 medium onion, peeled and finely chopped
100 g (4 oz) unsalted butter
3 garlic cloves, peeled and finely chopped
350 g (12 oz) peeled prawns (thawed if frozen)
2 tablespoons chopped fresh parsley
pinch of salt
freshly ground black pepper
pinch of cayenne
¼ teaspoon lemon juice
1 lemon, quartered, to garnish
hot crusty wholemeal rolls, to serve

Preparation and cooking time: 15 minutes, plus thawing if using frozen prawns

1. Fry the onion in the butter over moderate heat for 4 minutes, stirring once or twice. Add the garlic and prawns, stir well and lower the heat. Cook over low heat for 5 minutes, stirring occasionally.
2. Stir in half the parsley, and add salt, pepper, cayenne and lemon juice.
3. Serve hot, garnished with the remaining parsley and the lemon wedges. Serve with hot, crusty rolls.

Poached trout; Smoked mackerel and orange kebabs

PAN-FRIED DANISH EGG AND BACON

225 g (8 oz) streaky bacon rashers, rinded
4 large tomatoes, sliced
½ teaspoon mixed dried herbs
1 teaspoon vegetable oil
1 tablespoon plain flour
6 tablespoons milk
6 eggs
salt
freshly ground black pepper
15 g (½ oz) butter
sprigs of parsley, to garnish

Preparation and cooking time: 10 minutes

Pan-fried Danish egg and bacon

1. Place the bacon under a preheated medium grill, cook for 2 minutes and turn the rashers over.
2. Sprinkle the tomato halves with half the herbs and the oil and grill with the bacon for a further 3 minutes. Remove them from the heat and keep warm.
3. While the bacon and tomatoes are cooking, put the flour in a bowl, pour on the milk, stirring, then beat in the eggs. Add salt, pepper and the remaining mixed dried herbs.
4. Melt the butter in a small frying pan. When it foams, pour in the egg mixture and cook over moderately high heat for 4-5 minutes, lifting the edges occasionally with a spatula.
5. When the egg 'cake' is set, arrange the bacon rashers in a wheel pattern on top with the tomatoes overlapping round the edge. Garnish with the parsley sprigs and serve hot, straight from the pan in quarters.

APPLE HIVES

4 large cooking apples
4 tablespoons clear honey
75 g (3 oz) Cheddar cheese, grated
½ small lettuce, shredded
2 tablespoons walnut halves

Preparation and cooking time: 15 minutes

1. Line the grill pan with foil.
2. Peel and core the apples and cut each one across into 4 rings. Arrange them close together on the foil and spread them with half the honey.
3. Place under a preheated hot grill and cook for 3 minutes. Using a spatula or fish slice, turn over the apple rings, spread them with the remaining honey and grill for a further 3 minutes. Sprinkle the cheese over the slices and grill for 2 minutes more.
4. Re-form the slices into 4 apple shapes. Serve them on a bed of lettuce, topped by the walnut halves.

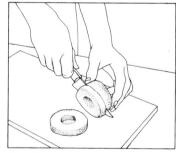

Cut the apple into 4 rings

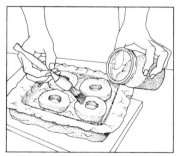

Spread with half the honey

Once grilled on both sides, sprinkle with cheese

When fully cooked, reassemble the rings

SPAGHETTI WITH CREAM SAUCE

350 g (12 oz) wholewheat spaghetti
salt
50 g (2 oz) butter
175 g (6 oz) button mushrooms, sliced
2-3 tablespoons chopped fresh herbs (basil, chervil, marjoram, parsley, as available)
freshly ground black pepper
300 ml (½ pint) double cream
2 egg yolks
100 g (4 oz) double Gloucester cheese, grated

Preparation and cooking time: 15 minutes

1. Cook the spaghetti in boiling water for 12-13 minutes, or according to the directions on the packet, until it is just tender. Melt the butter and gently fry the mushrooms over moderate heat for 4 minutes. Stir in 2 tablespoons of the herbs, add salt and pepper, and cook for a further minute.
3. In a separate pan gently heat the cream without allowing it to boil. Beat in the egg yolks, stir in the cheese, and add salt and pepper. Remove from the heat.
4. Drain the spaghetti, return it to the pan and toss it with the mushroom mixture. Turn the pasta into a warmed serving dish and pour on the cream and cheese sauce. Sprinkle with the reserved herbs, if using. Serve at once.

EGGS WITH BLUE CHEESE MAYONNAISE

6 eggs
200 ml (⅓ pint) mayonnaise
50 g (2 oz) Danish blue cheese
50 g (2 oz) Wensleydale cheese
6 tablespoons double cream
freshly ground black pepper
1 small lettuce
1 bunch watercress, trimmed
2 tablespoons chopped mint
2 tomatoes, quartered, to garnish

Preparation and cooking time: 15 minutes

1. Hard-boil the eggs, shell and halve them.
2. Place the mayonnaise in a bowl, grate and crumble in the cheeses and stir in the cream. Sprinkle lightly with pepper.
3. Shred the lettuce finely and toss it with the watercress sprigs and mint.
4. Divide the salad between 4 individual plates, arrange 3 egg halves on each, cut sides down, and spoon on the mayonnaise. Garnish with the tomato wedges.

BACON STEAKS WITH CUCUMBER SAUCE

4 bacon steaks
1 teaspoon vegetable oil
Sauce:
1 medium cucumber, peeled and diced
salt
20 g (¾ oz) butter
20 g (¾ oz) plain flour
300 ml (½ pint) milk
2 tablespoons double cream
1 tablespoon chopped chives
freshly ground black pepper
pinch of cayenne

Preparation and cooking time: 15 minutes

1. Brush the bacon steaks with oil and cook them under a preheated moderate grill for 4-5 minutes on each side. While they are cooking, make the sauce.
2. Cook the diced cucumber in boiling, salted water for 3 minutes, then drain it thoroughly and toss on kitchen paper to dry.
3. Melt the butter, stir in the flour and stir over moderate heat for 30 seconds. Gradually pour on the milk, stirring all the time, and bring the sauce to the boil. Simmer for 3 minutes. Stir the cucumber, cream and chives into the sauce, and add salt, pepper and cayenne to taste.
4. Spoon a little of the sauce on to the bacon steaks to garnish and serve the rest separately.
5. Small new potatoes and a green vegetable, such as broccoli spears, will cook in the same time.

LIVER WITH FRESH SAGE

450 g (1 lb) calves' or lambs' liver, cut into thin slices and then into 1 cm (½ inch) strips
1½ tablespoons plain flour
salt
freshly ground black pepper
½ teaspoon dried sage or 1 teaspoon finely chopped fresh sage
25 g (1 oz) butter
1 tablespoon vegetable oil
about 12 fresh sage leaves
120 ml (4 fl oz) condensed consommé
1 teaspoon lemon juice
4 sage sprigs, to garnish

Preparation and cooking time: 15 minutes

TURKEY IN SWEET AND SOUR SAUCE

4 portions of turkey breast, about 450 g (1 lb) total weight, cut into 5 × 1 cm (2 × ½ inch) strips
2 teaspoons cornflour
2 tablespoons vegetable oil
100 g (4 oz) mushrooms, thinly sliced
15 g (½ oz) butter
Sauce:
1½ teaspoons cornflour
6 tablespoons water
1½ tablespoons soft light brown sugar
1½ tablespoons clear honey
3 tablespoons red wine vinegar
3 tablespoons tomato purée
3 tablespoons orange juice
3 tablespoons soy sauce
salt

Preparation and cooking time: 15 minutes

1. Toss the turkey strips in the cornflour and fry them in oil, stirring occasionally, over moderately high heat for 3 minutes. Remove the meat and toss it on kitchen paper.
2. To make the sauce, stir the water on to the cornflour to make a smooth paste and stir in all the remaining sauce ingredients. Bring the sauce to the boil, stirring. Simmer for 1 minute, still stirring, then add the turkey. Simmer for 5 minutes over low heat.
3. Fry the mushrooms in the butter for 2 minutes over moderate heat, then stir them into the sauce. Serve hot, with rice.

1. Toss the liver strips in the flour seasoned with salt, pepper and the dried sage. Fry the coated liver in the butter and oil over moderate heat for 2 minutes. Turn the liver, add the sage leaves and cook for a further 2 minutes. Transfer the liver to a serving dish and discard the sage leaves.
2. Add the consommé and lemon juice to the pan, increase the heat and bring the sauce quickly to the boil, stirring. Taste and add salt and pepper. Garnish with the sage sprigs.
3. As a good accompaniment, you could cook a pan of long-grain rice at the same time, then the meat and rice should be ready together.

CLOCKWISE FROM TOP LEFT: Liver with fresh sage; Turkey in sweet and sour sauce; Bacon steaks with cucumber sauce

STEAK WITH ANCHOVIES

750 g (1½ lb) rump steak, cut into 4 pieces
freshly ground black pepper
40 g (1½ oz) butter, softened
1 tablespoon vegetable oil
1 tablespoon chopped fresh parsley
2 drops lemon juice
1 × 50 g (1¾ oz) can anchovy fillets, drained

Preparation and cooking time: 15 minutes

1. Snip the fat on the steak to prevent it from curling and grind pepper on to both sides.
2. Heat a frying pan over high heat. Add 15 g (½ oz) of the butter with the oil and, when it is very hot, add the steak. Seal the steak on one side for 2 minutes, turn and seal the other side for 2 minutes.
3. Reduce the heat to moderately hot and continue cooking for a further 1-3 minutes on each side, or until the steak is cooked as you like it.
4. While the meat is cooking, beat the remaining butter with the parsley, lemon juice and pepper. Shape it into a roll and chill it in the freezing compartment of the refrigerator for a few minutes.
5. To serve, arrange the anchovy fillets on the steak and, at the last moment, place pats of the parsley butter on top.
6. Spinach stirred with soured cream and spiced with grated nutmeg is a good, fast-cooking accompaniment.

Steak with anchovies

EVESHAM RAREBIT WITH MUSHROOMS

4 large slices of bread
175 g (6 oz) button mushrooms, sliced
50 g (2 oz) butter
1 tablespoon chopped fresh parsley
25 g (1 oz) plain flour
150 ml (¼ pint) brown ale or sweet cider
2 teaspoons prepared mustard
1 teaspoon mushroom ketchup (optional)
225 g (8 oz) strong Cheddar cheese, grated
2 eggs, lightly beaten
salt
freshly ground black pepper
pinch of cayenne

Preparation and cooking time: 15 minutes

1. Toast the bread on both sides under a preheated grill.
2. Gently fry the mushrooms in half of the butter over low heat for 5 minutes. Stir in the parsley and remove from the heat.
3. Melt the remaining butter over moderately low heat, stir in the flour and cook for 1 minute. Gradually add the ale or cider, still stirring, and bring to the boil. Simmer for 2 minutes. Remove the pan from the heat. Stir in the mustard, mushroom ketchup, if used, cheese, eggs and add salt, pepper and cayenne to taste.
4. Spoon the mushrooms over the 4 pieces of toast and cover them with the cheese mixture. Place under the preheated grill until brown and bubbling.

Variations:

This melt-in-the-mouth savoury is delicious with other fast foods, too. Instead of the mushrooms, top the toast with slices of ham, or with thawed frozen prawns, then cover them with the rarebit and brown under the grill. Or serve the rarebit with grilled bacon and tomatoes – cooked in a trice once the grill is hot – or with poached eggs.

CHIPOLATA AND PRUNE ROLLS

225 g (8 oz) chipolatas
350 g (12 oz) streaky bacon, rinded
8 prunes, stoned
4 pieces of pitta bread, split and warmed

Preparation and cooking time: 15 minutes

1. Twist each sausage in half and cut it into two.
2. Stretch the bacon rashers with the back of a knife and cut each one into three.
3. Wrap each sausage half and stoned prune in a piece of bacon. Secure each 2 or 3 rolls on a wooden cocktail stick – or use kitchen skewers.
4. Place the rolls under a preheated hot grill and cook for about 5-6 minutes, turning them once, until the bacon is crisp.
5. Remove the sticks and divide the sausage and prune rolls between the pieces of pitta. Serve hot.

Twist each chipolata in half to make 2 smaller sausages

Stretch the bacon using a knife along the length

Remove the stones from the prunes

Secure the sausage, prune and bacon rolls with a skewer

BANANA AND RUM FLAMBÉ

40 g (1½ oz) butter
4 ripe bananas, peeled and halved lengthwise
40 g (1½ oz) soft light brown sugar
2 tablespoons blanched almonds
2 tablespoons rum

Preparation and cooking time: 10 minutes

1. Melt the butter in a shallow flameproof dish, add the bananas in a single layer and sprinkle on the sugar and almonds.
2. Fry the bananas over moderate heat for about 3 minutes, then turn them and fry them until they are golden brown on the other side.
3. Warm the rum, pour it over the bananas, set it alight and serve at once. Chilled whipped cream is a delicious contrast.

RASPBERRY CREAM

300 ml (½ pint) double or whipping cream, chilled
50 g (2 oz) caster sugar
1 tablespoon Marsala (optional)
2 egg whites
225 g (8 oz) fresh raspberries, or frozen raspberries, thawed
50 g (2 oz) ratafia biscuits

Preparation time: 10 minutes, plus thawing if using frozen raspberries

1. Whip the cream until it is stiff. Stir in the sugar and the Marsala, if used.
2. Whisk the egg whites until they are stiff and fold them into the cream.
3. Reserve a few berries to decorate. Just before serving, stir the raspberries and ratafia biscuits into the cream. Spoon into 4 serving glasses and decorate with the reserved fruit.

GINGER SOUFFLÉ OMELETTE

6 eggs, separated
3 tablespoons caster sugar
25 g (1 oz) butter
2 small pieces preserved stem ginger, chopped
4 tablespoons ginger marmalade
1 tablespoon icing sugar, sifted

Preparation and cooking time: 15 minutes

1. Beat the egg yolks with the sugar. Whisk the egg whites until they are stiff, then fold into the egg yolk mixture.
2. Melt the butter in a large frying pan and pour in the egg mixture, spreading it to cover the base of the pan evenly. Cook the omelette over moderate heat for about 3 minutes, or until the base is golden brown.
3. Stir the chopped ginger into the marmalade.
4. Place the omelette under a preheated moderately hot grill for 2 minutes or until the omelette is firm and brown on top. Spread on the marmalade mixture and put under the grill for a further 1 minute.
5. Decorate the top with the sifted icing sugar. Serve very hot, cut in wedges.
6. Alternatively, you can cook the omelette in two batches in a small pan.

FRUITY YOGURT MALLOW

2 tablespoons soft light brown sugar
2 egg whites, stiffly whisked
300 ml (10 fl oz) plain unsweetened yogurt
2 tablespoons mixed dried fruits – sultanas, raisins, chopped dates
1 tablespoon chopped candied peel
2 tablespoons chopped hazelnuts
1 large banana, peeled and chopped
1 teaspoon lemon juice

Preparation time: 10 minutes

1. Gently fold the sugar into the egg whites, then fold in the yogurt. Take care not to break down the trapped air.
2. Fold in the dried fruits and most of the nuts, reserving a few to decorate. Toss the banana in the lemon juice and lastly fold this into the mixture.
3. Divide the dessert carefully between 4 serving glasses and decorate each one with a sprinkling of the reserved nuts on the top.
4. Chill the mallow for a few minutes before serving. It is best made only a short time before the meal.
5. Flavoured yogurts give delicious results, too – hazelnut and peach yogurts are specially good with added fruit and nuts.

IN THIRTY MINUTES

QUICK-FRIED PIZZA

225 g (8 oz) self-raising flour
½ teaspoon salt
freshly ground black pepper
½ teaspoon mixed dried herbs
4 tablespoons olive oil
4 tablespoons water
Topping:
4 tablespoons tomato purée
225 g (8 oz) tomatoes, skinned and thickly sliced
2 teaspoons chopped fresh basil, or parsley
225 g (8 oz) salami, skinned and thinly sliced
12 stuffed olives, sliced
100 g (4 oz) Gruyère cheese, thinly sliced

Preparation and cooking time: 30 minutes

1. Sift together the flour, salt and pepper and stir in the herbs. Stir in 2 tablespoons of the oil and all the water and mix to form a soft dough.
2. Turn on to a floured board and knead to remove the cracks. Roll the dough to a 23 cm (9 inch) circle.
3. Heat 1 tablespoon of the remaining oil in a large frying pan and cook the pizza base over moderate heat for 5 minutes. Remove the pizza from the pan, heat the remaining oil and return the pizza to cook the other side for 5 minutes.
4. When the pizza is golden brown on both sides, remove the pan from the heat. Spread the tomato purée over the top and cover it with sliced tomatoes. Sprinkle on the herbs.
5. Arrange the salami in overlapping rings, with the olives between them. Arrange the cheese slices on top, so that they do not completely cover the salami.
6. Cook the pizza under a preheated hot grill for 5 minutes, or until the cheese is sizzling and brown. Serve hot.

Variation

Pizzas are like toasted open sandwiches – no matter which variety of topping you choose, they are all equally delicious.

For a change, try making Seafood pizza. Cook the dough as described and cover it with the tomato purée, sliced tomatoes and chopped herb. Instead of the salami, arrange 100 g (4 oz) drained canned or bottled mussels or smoked oysters and 100 g (4 oz) peeled prawns. Grind on plenty of black pepper, add a pinch of cayenne and top with the olives and – in this case – grated cheese.

MELON, PIMENTO AND HAM SALAD

150 ml (¼ pint) mayonnaise
1 tablespoon soured cream
2 canned pimentos, drained
1 tablespoon tomato purée
salt
freshly ground black pepper
225 g (8 oz) cooked ham, diced
100 g (4 oz) seedless green grapes
2 tablespoons walnut halves
1 small ogen melon, chilled
a few lettuce leaves, to garnish

Preparation and cooking time: 30 minutes

1. To make the sauce, put the mayonnaise, cream, pimentos, tomato purée, salt and pepper into a blender and blend until smooth.
2. Toss the diced ham, grapes and walnut halves in the pimento sauce.
3. Cut the melon in half, discard the seeds and scoop out the flesh, using a vegetable baller. Or cut the flesh away from the rind and cut it into strips.
4. Cover a serving dish with lettuce leaves, arrange the ham salad in the centre and surround it with a ring of melon balls or strips.
5. Diced cooked chicken is equally nice served this way, and blends very well with the pimento sauce.

To make a melon bowl
For a special presentation, you can use the melon shell as a container – it looks specially attractive filled with fruit salad or frosty fruit sorbet decorated with sprigs of mint.

Cut a thin slice from one side and scoop out the flesh, discarding the seeds. Trim the flesh away from the melon skin to leave thin 'walls' – a grapefruit knife with a curved blade is a help. Cut zig-zag points around the top of the shell. Pile in the salad to make a mound.

Quick-fried pizza; Melon, pimento and ham salad

MUMBLED EGGS WITH PEPPERS

1 green pepper, halved, cored and seeded
6 slices of bread
8 eggs
2 teaspoons prepared mustard
salt
freshly ground black pepper
15 g (½ oz) butter
100 g (4 oz) full fat soft cheese
2 tablespoons single cream

Preparation and cooking time: 20 minutes

1. Place the pepper cut side down and cook under a preheated hot grill for 4-5 minutes, until the skin turns black and bubbly. Cool it in water, peel off the skin and cut lengthways into thin strips.
2. Toast the bread and cut each slice into 4 triangles. If preferred, remove the crusts.
3. Beat the eggs and mustard together, and add salt and pepper.
4. Melt the butter, add the egg mixture and stir over moderate heat for 3-4 minutes, until beginning to set.
5. Stir in the cheese and cook for about 2 minutes more, until the mixture is softly set. Stir in the cream.
6. Pile the egg mixture into a dish, arrange the toast round it and criss-cross the pepper strips on top. Serve at once.

STIR-FRIED CHICKEN

4 breasts of chicken
2 tablespoons cornflour
3 tablespoons soy sauce
5 tablespoons vegetable oil
2 garlic cloves, peeled and finely chopped
4 green peppers, cored, seeded and sliced
3 tablespoons blanched almonds
salt
freshly ground black pepper

Preparation and cooking time: 25 minutes

1. Cut the chicken flesh into dice. Toss it in the cornflour and stir in 2 tablespoons of the soy sauce and 2 tablespoons of the oil.
2. Fry the garlic, green peppers and almonds in the remaining oil over moderate heat for 3-4 minutes. Lift from the oil with a draining spoon and keep warm.
3. Drain the chicken and stir-fry in the oil for 4-5 minutes, until the meat is just firm.
4. Return the peppers and almonds to the pan and stir in the remaining soy sauce. Add salt and pepper to taste, if necessary. Serve hot.
5. Noodles stirred with plenty of butter and chopped parsley are a good accompaniment.

SAVOURY SODA BREAD AND COTTAGE CHEESE SALAD

225 g (8 oz) plain wholemeal flour
225 g (8 oz) plain flour
1 teaspoon salt
2 teaspoons baking powder
1 teaspoon bicarbonate of soda
50 g (2 oz) butter or hard margarine, grated
1 tablespoon chopped fresh herbs (e.g. parsley, chervil or marjoram), or 2 teaspoons dried herbs
75 g (3 oz) Cheddar cheese, grated
about 300 ml (½ pint) milk
2 teaspoons lemon juice
French dressing:
4 tablespoons olive oil
1 tablespoon cider vinegar
¼ teaspoon mustard powder
salt
freshly ground black pepper
Salad:
1 small curly endive or lettuce, shredded
1 bunch watercress, trimmed
2 heads chicory, sliced
225 g (8 oz) cottage cheese

Preparation and cooking time: 30 minutes
Oven: 220°C, 425°F, Gas Mark 7

1. Sift together the flours, salt, baking powder and soda, and tip in the bran remaining in the sieve. Stir in the butter or margarine, the herbs and cheese. Mix together the milk and lemon juice, and pour on enough to mix to a soft dough. Knead lightly in the bowl.
2. Divide the dough into 4 equal pieces and shape each one into a round ball shape. Place them on a greased and floured baking sheet, slightly flatten the tops and cut 2 parallel slashes in the top of each.
3. Bake in a preheated oven for about 20 minutes, or until the loaves sound hollow when tapped underneath.
4. Meanwhile, whisk together the ingredients for the French dressing or put them into a lidded jar and shake them vigorously.
5. Mix together the lettuce, watercress sprigs and chicory. Just before serving, toss them with the French dressing. Arrange the salad on a plate with the cottage cheese in the centre. Serve with the warm soda bread, and butter.

Mumbled eggs with peppers; Stir-fried chicken

PORK IN ORANGE AND GINGER SAUCE

750 g (1½ lb) pork fillet (tenderloin)
4 teaspoons plain flour
salt
freshly ground black pepper
¼ teaspoon dried thyme
25 g (1 oz) butter
2 oranges
2 tablespoons ginger syrup
2 pieces preserved stem ginger, thinly sliced
4 tablespoons double cream

Preparation and cooking time: 30 minutes

1. Cut the pork into 2.5 cm (1 inch) slices and toss them in the flour mixed with salt and pepper and dried thyme.
2. Fry the pork in the butter over high heat for 2 minutes on each side. Reduce the heat to moderate, cover the pan (using foil if it has no lid) and cook for a further 5 minutes on each side.
3. Squeeze the juice and grate the rind of 1 orange.
4. Remove the pork from the pan, stir in about 2 tablespoons orange juice and rind, then the ginger syrup and sliced ginger, and add salt and pepper. Add the cream and allow it just to heat, without boiling.
5. Pour the sauce over the meat and garnish with the remaining orange, cut into 8 wedges.
6. Serve with a bowl of boiled rice and a green salad or – delicious with the rich sauce – spinach.

Oranges and lemons
Do you know how to extract the last drop of juice from an orange or lemon? Put the fruit on a table and, using the flat palm of your hand, roll it firmly backwards and forwards a few times. This releases the juice and ensures none is wasted.

Before peeling the fruit, dunk it for a few seconds in boiling water – this loosens the peel and makes the job quicker, easier and less messy.

The same tip works for apples – dip them in boiling water to skin more easily.

MARINATED BACON CHOPS

4 bacon chops
200 ml (⅓ pint) light ale
3 medium onions, peeled and sliced
1 bay leaf
6 black peppercorns
1 tablespoon black treacle
1 tablespoon lemon juice
freshly ground black pepper
2 tablespoons vegetable oil

Preparation and cooking time: 25 minutes, plus at least 2 hours' marinating

1. Place the chops in a dish with the ale, one sliced onion, the bay leaf and peppercorns. Cover and leave in the refrigerator for 2 hours, or more.
2. Remove the chops from the marinade and strain the sauce into a pan. Bring the sauce to the boil and boil over high heat for about 4 minutes, or until it has reduced by half.
3. Stir in the treacle and lemon juice and add pepper. When the treacle has melted, remove from the heat.
4. Brush one side of the chops with the sauce and cook them under a preheated hot grill for 4-5 minutes. Turn the chops, brush the other side with sauce and cook for a further 4-5 minutes.
5. Fry the remaining onions in the oil for 2 minutes over moderate heat, add the remaining sauce and simmer for 5 minutes.
6. Pour the glazed onions over the chops to serve. A fresh salad makes a cool, crisp contrast.

Marinating
Here's a simple way to marinate meat and fish. It's especially suitable when you are steeping a piece of meat that is an awkward shape, such as a leg of lamb or a whole chicken, or cubes of meat or fish that need to be turned frequently.

Put all the marinating ingredients into a plastic bag (first checking that there's no hole in it!). Put in the meat or fish and tie it securely with a twist-tie. Just turn the bag over every now and then, to distribute the flavour evenly.

CRISPY-COATED LIVER

75 g (3 oz) butter
1 large onion, peeled and sliced into rings
25 g (1 oz) plain flour
salt
freshly ground black pepper
½ teaspoon mixed dried herbs
1 egg
1 tablespoon milk
450 g (1 lb) lambs' liver, thinly sliced diagonally
50 g (2 oz) rolled porridge oats
120 ml (4 fl oz) medium sherry
120 ml (4 fl oz) chicken stock
sprigs of parsley, to garnish

Preparation and cooking time: 25 minutes

Crispy-coated liver

1. Melt 25 g (1 oz) of the butter in a frying-pan and fry the onion rings over moderate heat for 5-6 minutes, turning them occasionally. Remove the onion rings from the pan and keep them warm.
2. Mix the flour with salt and pepper and stir in the dried herbs. Beat together the egg and milk. Dry the liver slices on kitchen paper. Dip them first into the seasoned flour to coat them on both sides, then into the egg and milk and finally, in the oats. Press the oats firmly to make an even coating.
3. Melt the remaining butter in the pan and when hot, and the foaming has subsided, fry the liver slices over moderate heat for about 3 minutes on each side, until the coating is crisp and brown. The liver should be still pink inside – test it by piercing with the point of a sharp knife.
4. Remove the liver from the pan and keep it warm. Tip in any remaining seasoned flour and stir well. Pour on the sherry and stock, bring to the boil, stirring, and add salt and pepper to taste.
5. Arrange the liver on a heated serving dish, scatter the onion rings on top and pour over the sauce.

LAMB CHOPS WITH VEGETABLE KEBABS

75 g (3 oz) butter, softened
1 teaspoon paprika
1 teaspoon tomato purée
¼ teaspoon Worcestershire sauce
salt
freshly ground black pepper
4 loin of lamb chops
3 tablespoons vegetable oil
1 tablespoon red wine vinegar
4 small courgettes, cut into 2 cm (¾ inch) slices
100 g (4 oz) small button mushrooms
1 red or yellow pepper, cored, seeded and cut into 3 cm
    (1¼ inch) squares

Preparation time: 30 minutes

1. Beat together the butter, paprika, tomato purée, Worcestershire sauce, salt and pepper.
2. Use half of this to spread on both sides of the chops. Shape the remainder into 8 pats and chill.
3. Mix together the oil and vinegar, add plenty of salt and pepper, and toss the courgettes, mushrooms and green pepper in this dressing. Drain the vegetables and thread them on to 4 small skewers.
4. Cook the chops under a preheated hot grill for 1 minute on each side. Reduce the heat to moderately hot and place the kebabs under the grill. Cook for 5-6 minutes, turning the chops and skewers once and basting the kebabs with the remaining oil and vinegar.
5. Serve the chops each with 2 pats of paprika butter.

PLAICE IN SWEET AND SOUR SAUCE

4 fillets of plaice, about 175 g (6 oz) each
100 g (4 oz) button mushrooms, sliced
1 red pepper, cored, seeded and very thinly sliced
2 tablespoons flaked blanched almonds
Sauce:
1 tablespoon cornflour
4 tablespoons orange juice
grated rind of 1 orange
1 tablespoon soft light brown sugar
1 tablespoon clear honey
1 tablespoon cider vinegar
1 tablespoon tomato purée
1 tablespoon soy sauce
1 tablespoon sweet sherry
1 tablespoon vegetable oil
1 teaspoon Tabasco sauce
salt
freshly ground black pepper

Preparation and cooking time: 20 minutes

TROUT WITH APPLES

4 large rainbow trout, cleaned
freshly ground black pepper
1 tablespoon lemon juice
4 sprigs rosemary
50 g (2 oz) butter
2 dessert apples, cored and thickly sliced
To garnish:
1 lemon, quartered
1 teaspoon chopped fresh parsley

Preparation and cooking time: 25 minutes

1. Sprinkle the inside of the trout with plenty of pepper and the lemon juice and place a sprig of rosemary in the cavity. (Use a pinch of dried rosemary if the fresh herb is not available.)
2. Fry the trout in the butter over moderate heat for 6 minutes. Using wooden spatulas or fish slices, turn the fish over, taking care not to break the skin. Add the apples. Cook for a further 6-8 minutes, turning the apples once, until the fish are just cooked and the apples are deep golden brown. Transfer to a warm serving dish.
3. Serve the fish surrounded by the apples and garnished with the lemon wedges dipped, along the edges, in the parsley.
4. The trout does not need a sauce, as the apples are moist and full of flavour. Broccoli spears with melted butter or, if you have time, hollandaise sauce are a lovely accompaniment.

1. Cut 4 pieces of foil 20 × 30 cm (8 × 12 inches) and brush the centres with a little oil. Trim the fish and arrange each fillet on a piece of foil. Scatter the mushrooms, pepper and almonds over them. Bring up the sides of the foil to make a dish shape.
2. To make the sauce, put the cornflour into a bowl and gradually stir in the orange juice. Stir in all the remaining sauce ingredients. Taste and adjust the seasoning if necessary.
3. Pour the sauce over the fish. Fold and seal the edges of the foil firmly to make watertight parcels. Place them in a steamer or colander over a pan of boiling water for 20 minutes.
4. Serve the fish in the foil parcels if desired.
5. While the fish is cooking put on a pan of rice or noodles, to be ready at the same time.

Plaice in sweet and sour sauce

PEACH CARAMELS

1 tablespoon ground almonds
2-3 drops almond essence
1 tablespoon caster sugar
150 ml (5 fl oz) double or whipping cream, stiffly whipped
4 large ripe peaches, skinned, halved and stoned
2 tablespoons blanched almonds, toasted
Sauce:
100 g (4 oz) soft light brown sugar
25 g (1 oz) butter
1 tablespoon milk

Preparation and cooking time: 20 minutes

1. Stir the ground almonds, almond essence and caster sugar into the whipped cream.
2. Fill the peach cavities with almond cream, reserving a little for decoration. Sandwich the peach halves together and arrange on a serving dish.
3. Bring the brown sugar, butter and milk to the boil and simmer over low heat for exactly 7 minutes. Remove from the heat and beat with a wooden spoon for 1 minute, until the sauce is smooth.
4. Pour the sauce over the peaches in 'waves', so that it does not cover them completely.
5. When the sauce has cooled (about 3 minutes) spoon or pipe the remaining cream over and scatter with the toasted almonds.

DROP SCONES WITH BILBERRY SAUCE

Makes about 12
100 g (4 oz) plain flour
2 teaspoons baking powder
pinch of salt
1 egg, beaten
150 ml (¼ pint) milk
vegetable oil, for greasing
Sauce:
225 g (8 oz) frozen bilberries or blueberries
2 tablespoons blackberry (bramble) jelly
1 teaspoon lemon juice
about 1 tablespoon sugar (optional)
150 ml (5 fl oz) soured cream, to serve

Preparation and cooking time: 20 minutes

POACHED PEARS WITH CHOCOLATE SAUCE

450 ml (¾ pint) water
75 g (3 oz) sugar
¼ teaspoon vanilla essence
4 large ripe dessert pears, peeled
100 g (4 oz) plain bitter chocolate

Preparation and cooking time: 20-25 minutes

1. Bring the water, sugar and vanilla essence to the boil.
2. Poach the pears over moderately low heat for 5-10 minutes, turning them occasionally, until they are really tender. Carefully lift the pears from the syrup and keep them warm.
3. Break the chocolate into squares and melt it in the syrup over low heat. Beat the mixture well, then simmer for 10 minutes, until the sauce is thick enough to coat the spoon.
4. Serve the pears warm, with the sauce separately.
5. Alternatively, allow the pears to cool, then chill them. They are delicious with hot or cold chocolate sauce and plenty of whipped cream.

1. Sift together the flour, baking powder and salt, stir in the egg and gradually pour on the milk, beating all the time. Beat until the batter is smooth.
2. Lightly oil a heavy frying pan and when hot drop the batter on to it, 2 teaspoons at a time, well apart to allow for spreading.
3. Cook the scones over moderate heat for about 2-3 minutes, or until the surface starts to bubble. Flip them over and cook the other side for 2-3 minutes, until golden brown. Keep the drop scones warm in a clean, folded teatowel.
4. To make the sauce, stir together the bilberries, fruit jelly and lemon juice and bring to the boil. Simmer for 2 minutes. Taste and sweeten with the sugar, if necessary.
5. Serve the drop scones warm, and the sauce and soured cream separately.

Peach caramel; Poached pear with chocolate sauce; Drop scones with bilberry sauce

IN FORTY-FIVE MINUTES

GRILLED CHICKEN WITH CHEESE

4 breast pieces of chicken
4 tablespoons vegetable oil
1 tablespoon lemon juice
1 teaspoon dried thyme
salt
freshly ground black pepper
100 g (4 oz) cooked ham, thinly sliced
50 g (2 oz) Gruyère cheese, thinly sliced
2 large tomatoes, sliced

Preparation and cooking time: 45 minutes

1. Cut 4 pieces of foil about 30 cm (12 inches) square.
2. Skin the chicken pieces and cut 3 slits in each chicken breast. Lay on the foil.
3. Mix together the oil, lemon juice and thyme, salt and pepper.
4. Draw the foil round the chicken, pour on the sauce and seal the parcels.
5. Cook the chicken parcels under a preheated moderate grill, turning them once, for 35 minutes until the juices run clear when the chicken pieces are pierced with a skewer. It is important to check that if using an electric grill the foil does not touch the element. Increase the heat to high.
6. Open the parcels, arrange the sliced ham, then cheese, then tomatoes on the chicken breasts and spoon a little sauce on to the tomatoes. Grill the topping under high heat for about 3-4 minutes, until the cheese is bubbling.
7. For a really super accompaniment, try corn on the cob cooked in boiling water and then generously brushed with melted butter and pepper. A couple of minutes under the hot grill sizzles them to perfection.

VEAL AND MUSHROOM ROLLS

4 veal escalopes, about 75 g (3 oz) each
75 g (3 oz) butter
2 medium rashers unsmoked collar or back bacon, rinded and cut into 1 cm (½ inch) squares
50 g (2 oz) mushrooms, finely chopped
2 tablespoons sultanas
1 tablespoon chopped fresh parsley
2 tablespoons grated Cheddar cheese
salt
freshly ground black pepper
2 teaspoons plain flour
175 ml (6 fl oz) red wine
parsley sprigs, to garnish

Preparation and cooking time: 45 minutes

1. Flatten the escalopes with a rolling pin and cut each one in half.
2. Melt 25 g (1 oz) of the butter in a pan and fry the bacon over moderate heat for 3 minutes, stirring once or twice. Add the mushrooms and cook for a further 2 minutes. Stir in the sultanas, parsley and cheese, and add salt and pepper. Remove from the heat.
3. Divide the filling between the pieces of veal and press it well down. Roll up the veal, Swiss-roll style, and tie each one round with thin string to secure.
4. Melt the remaining butter in the pan and fry the veal rolls over moderate heat for about 8 minutes, turning them to brown them evenly.
5. Remove the veal from the pan, stir in the flour and pour on the wine. Bring to the boil, and add salt and pepper to taste. Return the veal. Cover the pan and simmer over low heat for 10 minutes, turning once. Remove the strings and garnish with the parsley.

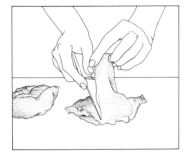

Remove the skin from the chicken breasts

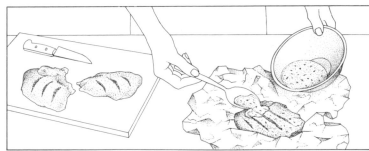

Make 3 slits in the chicken breast. Raise the sides of the foil round the chicken to contain the sauce

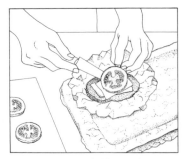

Open foil carefully and top with ham, cheese and tomato

Grilled chicken with cheese; Veal and mushroom rolls

CARROT CRUMBLE

450 g (1 lb) carrots, peeled
salt
15 g (½ oz) butter
2 teaspoons clear honey
3 tablespoons chicken stock
freshly ground black pepper
1 × 225 g (8 oz) can sweetcorn, drained
1 tablespoon chopped fresh parsley
Topping:
100 g (4 oz) wholemeal flour
65 g (2½ oz) butter or hard margarine
25 g (1 oz) breadcrumbs
a pinch of ground ginger

Preparation and cooking time: 40 minutes
Oven: 190°C, 375°F, Gas Mark 5

1. Cook the carrots in boiling, salted water for
15 minutes, or until they are just tender.
2. Drain and dice them, stir in the butter, honey and
chicken stock with salt and pepper to taste.
3. Spread the carrots in a greased 1 litre (2 pint)
baking dish. Cover with the sweetcorn and sprinkle
on the parsley.
4. To make the topping, mix the flour with ½
teaspoon salt and rub in the butter or margarine until
the mixture is like crumbs. Stir in the breadcrumbs
and ginger.
5. Sprinkle the topping over the vegetables and cook
in a preheated oven for 20 minutes, until the crumble
is crisp and brown. Serve hot. A green vegetable such
as broccoli in parsley sauce is a good accompaniment.

BACON AND SWEETCORN CHOWDER

100 g (4 oz) streaky bacon rashers, rinded and diced
50 g (2 oz) butter
1 medium onion, peeled and sliced
1 medium leek, peeled and sliced
2 sticks celery, sliced
2 medium carrots, peeled and thinly sliced
300 ml (½ pint) chicken stock
225 g (8 oz) potatoes, peeled and diced
1 × 425 g (15 oz) can sweetcorn kernels, drained
450 ml (¾ pint) milk
salt
freshly ground black pepper
a pinch of cayenne
6 tablespoons double cream
1 tablespoon chopped fresh parsley, to garnish

Preparation and cooking time: 45 minutes

1. Fry the bacon in half the butter over moderate heat
for 2-3 minutes.
2. Add the onion, leek, celery and carrot, stir well
and cook for 4 minutes.
3. Pour on the stock, bring to the boil and add the
potatoes. Return the stock to the boil, cover the pan
and simmer for 20 minutes.
4. Add the sweetcorn and milk and bring to
simmering point. Simmer for 3 minutes and add salt,
pepper and cayenne.
5. Stir in the cream and allow just to heat through,
then stir in the remaining butter. Garnish with the
parsley and serve very hot.
6. Serve with plenty of hot, crusty rolls.

CHEESE AND OLIVE PUFF BALLS

225 g (8 oz) Cheddar cheese, grated
2 eggs, separated
2 tablespoons light ale
¼ teaspoon salt
freshly ground black pepper
50 g (2 oz) plain flour
1 teaspoon baking powder
24 stuffed olives
oil for deep frying
Salad:
225 g (8 oz) firm tomatoes, sliced
2 spring onions, peeled and sliced
1 tablespoon chopped fresh basil
4 tablespoons French Dressing (page 23)
1 tablespoon soured cream

**Preparation and cooking time: 45 minutes, plus
30 minutes standing**

1. Beat together the cheese, egg yolks and ale in a mixing bowl and add salt and pepper.
2. Sift the flour and baking powder and stir them into the cheese mixture.
3. Whisk the egg whites until stiff and fold them into the mixture. Cover the bowl and leave to stand for 30 minutes.
4. To make the salad, arrange the tomato slices in a dish and sprinkle them with the onions and basil. Mix together the French dressing and soured cream and pour over the salad.
5. Dust your hands with flour and divide the cheese mixture into 24 balls, slightly larger than a large walnut. Push an olive gently in the centre of each one and shape the cheese mixture round it so that it is enclosed.
6. Heat the oil in a pan and when it is smoking, fry the cheese balls, a few at a time, for 2-3 minutes, until they are puffed and golden. Drain them on kitchen paper and serve at once.

BLUE CHEESE PUDDING

1 small onion, peeled and chopped
50 g (2 oz) butter
50 g (2 oz) plain flour
300 ml (½ pint) milk
50 g (2 oz) Danish blue cheese, crumbled
50 g (2 oz) cottage cheese
salt
freshly ground black pepper
4 large eggs, separated
50 g (2 oz) breadcrumbs
2 tablespoons chopped fresh parsley
4 large tomatoes, sliced
1 teaspoon vegetable oil
Salad:
1 bunch watercress, trimmed
1 small cucumber, diced
1 tablespoon chopped chives
1 tablespoon clear honey
4 tablespoons French Dressing (page 23)

Preparation and cooking time: 45 minutes
Oven: 190°C, 375°F, Gas Mark 5

1. Fry the onion in the butter over moderate heat for
3 minutes, stirring once or twice.
2. Stir in the flour and gradually pour on the milk,
still stirring. Bring to the boil and simmer for
2 minutes.
3. Beat in the cheeses and add salt and pepper.
4. Remove from the heat and beat in the egg yolks,
breadcrumbs and parsley.
5. Whisk the egg whites until they are stiff, then fold
them into the mixture.
6. Spread half the mixture into a greased 1 litre
(2 pint) baking dish. Cover with half the tomato slices,
then spread on the remaining cheese mixture.
Arrange the remaining tomato slices on top and
sprinkle them with the oil.
6. Bake in a preheated oven for 30 minutes. The
pudding should be just firm to the touch.
7. Toss the watercress sprigs, cucumber and chives
together. Stir the honey into the French dressing and,
just before serving, toss in the salad.

MIXED VEGETABLE CURRY

1 small cauliflower, cut into florets
175 g (6 oz) carrots, peeled and diced
175 g (6 oz) potatoes, peeled and diced
salt
225 g (8 oz) broad beans
1 large onion, peeled and sliced
40 g (1½ oz) butter
1 tablespoon curry powder (mild or hot, to taste)
1 teaspoon curry paste
1 tablespoon plain flour
2 tablespoons mango chutney sauce
150 ml (5 fl oz) single cream
2 tablespoons blanched almonds
To garnish:
4 hard-boiled eggs, cut into wedges
pinch of paprika

Preparation and cooking time: 40 minutes

1. Steam the cauliflower, carrots and potatoes over
boiling, salted water for 10 minutes. Cook the broad
beans in boiling, salted water for 5 minutes.
2. Drain the vegetables, reserving the cooking liquid
from the broad beans and keep them warm.
3. Fry the onion in the butter over low heat for
5 minutes, stir in the curry powder and increase
the heat to moderate. Fry, stirring, for 1 minute.
4. Stir in the curry paste and flour and cook for
1 minute. Then add the chutney sauce.
5. Measure 600 ml (1 pint) of the vegetable stock, or
make it up to that amount with water or chicken
stock. Pour the stock gradually on to the curry
mixture, stirring, and bring to the boil. Simmer for
5 minutes, then stir in the cream.
6. Stir in the vegetables and allow them just to heat
through before serving. Stir in the almonds.
7. Serve the curry hot, garnished with the sliced eggs
and paprika. Boiled rice and grilled or fried
poppadoms will complete the meal.

Steaming vegetables
Steaming vegetables has distinct advantages over
cooking them in boiling water. More of the
precious nutrients are retained and more texture,
colour and flavour, too. It's a particularly good
method to choose when, as in the recipe for
Mixed vegetable curry, you want to cook or
partly cook several types of vegetables at once.
   To give the vegetables even more flavour, try
steaming them over chicken stock, and use it
afterwards for soup or sauce.
   You can buy an inexpensive collapsible
steamer that fits any saucepan, or improvise by
fitting a colander into a large pan.

SALAMI AND PASTA SALAD

100 g (4 oz) short-cut wholewheat macaroni
salt
225 g (8 oz) new potatoes, scrubbed but not scraped
1 recipe French Dressing (page 23)
3 spring onions, peeled and sliced
3 tablespoons walnut halves
100 g (4 oz) salami, skinned and diced
100 g (4 oz) coarse garlic sausage, skinned and diced
1 tablespoon chopped chives
6 tablespoons soured cream
1 teaspoon prepared mustard
freshly ground black pepper

Preparation and cooking time: 45 minutes, including cooling

1. Cook the macaroni in boiling, salted water for 12-13 minutes, or according to the instructions on the packet, until it is just tender. Drain it well.
2. At the same time, cook the potatoes in boiling, salted water for 12-15 minutes, or until they are just tender.
3. Drain the potatoes and, as soon as they are cool enough to handle, rub off the skins. Dice or quarter the potatoes if they are large.
4. While the pasta and potatoes are still hot, toss them in the French dressing. Set aside to cool.
5. When the pasta and potatoes are cool, stir in the spring onions, walnuts (reserving a few to garnish), the salami, garlic sausage and chives.
6. Stir together the soured cream and mustard and add plenty of pepper. Spoon the dressing on to the salad, and toss to coat it thoroughly.
7. Arrange the salad on a serving platter and garnish with the reserved walnuts.
8. Slices or cubes of chilled melon make a delightful contrast to this filling salad.

MARINATED SIRLOIN STEAK

750 g (1½ lb) sirloin steak
1 medium onion, peeled and thinly sliced
1 garlic clove, peeled and crushed
2 tablespoons olive oil
1 tablespoon tomato purée
1 tablespoon soy sauce
1 teaspoon Tabasco sauce
1 tablespoon soft dark brown sugar
2 tablespoons concentrated orange juice
salt
1 × 425 g (15 oz) can tomatoes
100 g (4 oz) mushrooms, thinly sliced
15 g (½ oz) butter
1 tablespoon chopped fresh parsley, to garnish

Preparation and cooking time: 45 minutes, plus extra marinating, if possible

1. Cut the steak into 4 portions, and trim to remove any excess fat.
2. Put into a bowl with the onion, garlic, oil, tomato purée, sauces, sugar, orange juice and salt. Stir the marinade well and turn the meat over and over to coat it thoroughly. Leave the steak in the marinade for a few minutes or a few hours, as convenient.
3. Turn the steak and marinade into a pan with the tomatoes, taste and adjust the seasoning if necessary. Bring to simmering point and simmer, uncovered, over moderate heat for 20-25 minutes, until the steak is tender and the sauce has thickened.
4. Fry the mushrooms in the butter and scatter them over the steak. Garnish with the parsley.
5. This is a good hearty meat dish, full of flavour. Plain boiled potatoes and a green vegetable such as cabbage, lightly simmered in chicken stock and flavoured with sesame or caraway seeds, make a good accompaniment.
6. When time is not quite so pressing, you can use a cheaper cut of meat for a dish that is nearly as good. Try using stewing steak or beef skirt and adjusting the time accordingly: 1½-2 hours after several hours of marinating. This makes a super supper party dish.

PRUNE-STUFFED FILLET OF PORK

2 small pork fillets (tenderloin) about 750 g (1½ lb) total weight
8 prunes, halved and stoned
2 tablespoons seedless raisins
3 tablespoons clear honey
15 g (½ oz) butter
1 teaspoon plain flour
150 ml (¼ pint) sweet cider
salt
freshly ground black pepper

Preparation and cooking time: 45 minutes

1. Trim the pork fillets and cut away the 'silver thread'. Cut them lengthways without cutting them right through.
2. Arrange the prune halves along one side of each fillet, cover the prunes with 1 tablespoon of the raisins and with 1 tablespoon of the honey. Close up the fillets again, enclosing the fruit, and secure with wooden cocktail sticks or tie with thin string.
3. Melt the butter in a pan and when it is hot fry the pork fillets until brown on both sides.
4. Stir in the flour, pour on the cider and bring to the boil.
5. Add salt and pepper, and the remaining raisins and simmer, covered, turning the pork once, for 30 minutes.
6. Remove the sticks or ties and spread the remaining honey along the fillets of pork. Glaze under a preheated hot grill for 2 minutes.
7. Plain boiled rice and green salad contrast well with the sweet, fruity sauce.

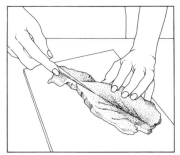
Slit the fillet lengthways to make a pocket for the stuffing

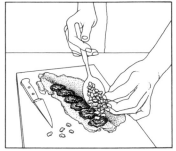
Arrange the stuffing in layers along the length

Fold over the top of the fillet so that the stuffing is enclosed

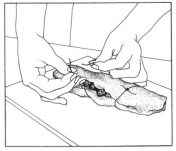
Tie the fillet together with string to secure the stuffing

LAMB CUTLETS ON A BED OF SPINACH

12 lamb cutlets
2 tablespoons vegetable oil
40 g (1½ oz) butter
1 kg (2 lb) fresh spinach
150 ml (5 fl oz) soured cream
1 teaspoon lemon juice
salt
freshly ground black pepper
1 lemon, quartered, to garnish

Preparation and cooking time: 45 minutes

1. Cut the meat away from the bones and trim off the fat. Shape each piece of meat into a circle and tie it firmly with fine string.
2. Heat the oil and 15 g (½ oz) of the butter and fry the medallions of lamb for 2 minutes on each side over high heat.
3. Reduce the heat to low and continue cooking for about 6 minutes on each side. The lamb should be crisp and brown on the outside, but pink and moist inside.
4. While the meat is cooking, wash the spinach and tear off the tough stalks. Cook the spinach in the water clinging to the leaves for 10 minutes, or until it is tender. Drain it in a colander, pressing out all excess moisture.
5. Return the spinach to the pan with the remaining butter and the soured cream and lemon juice. Add salt and pepper and stir over moderate heat until the spinach and cream forms a smooth, thick purée.
6. Spread the spinach purée on a serving dish, arrange the lamb on top and garnish with the lemon wedges.
7. Boiled new potatoes make the nicest possible accompaniment.

Prune-stuffed fillet of pork

PEAR AND GINGER SPONGE PUDDING

450 g (1 lb) dessert pears, peeled, cored and sliced
50 g (2 oz) soft light brown sugar
½ teaspoon ground ginger
2 pieces preserved stem ginger, thinly sliced
Sponge:
100 g (4 oz) self-raising flour
1 teaspoon ground ginger
50 g (2 oz) caster sugar
50 g (2 oz) shredded suet
1 egg
3 tablespoons milk

Preparation and cooking time: 40 minutes
Oven: 200°C, 400°F, Gas Mark 6

1. Arrange the pear slices in a 1 litre (2 pint)
ovenproof dish.
2. Mix together the sugar and the ground and sliced
ginger and sprinkle over the fruit.
3. To make the sponge, sift together the flour and
ground ginger and stir in the sugar and suet.
4. Beat in the egg and milk and beat the mixture until
it is smooth. Spoon over the fruit and level the top.
5. Bake in a preheated oven for 25 minutes, until the
sponge is firm but springy to the touch. Serve hot,
with cream or custard.

PEACHES IN MARMALADE SAUCE

4 large, ripe peaches, peeled, halved and stoned
4 tablespoons orange jelly marmalade
40 g (1½ oz) butter
¼ teaspoon ground cinnamon
2 tablespoons blanched almonds

Preparation and cooking time: 45 minutes
Oven: 180°C, 350°F, Gas Mark 4

1. Arrange the peach halves, cut sides up, in a
shallow baking dish.
2. Melt the marmalade, butter and cinnamon together
in a saucepan, then pour the sauce over the peaches.
Scatter with the nuts.
3. Cover with foil and cook in a preheated oven for
35 minutes. Serve hot, with chilled whipped cream.

LEFT TO RIGHT: Pear and ginger sponge pudding; Peaches in
marmalade sauce; Apple cobbler

APPLE COBBLER

450 g (1 lb) cooking apples, peeled, cored and thinly sliced
50 g (2 oz) soft light brown sugar
2 tablespoons orange juice
50 g (2 oz) stoned dates, chopped
2 firm bananas, thickly sliced
1 teaspoon lemon juice
Scone topping:
225 g (8 oz) plain flour
¼ teaspoon ground ginger
1 teaspoon bicarbonate of soda
1 teaspoon cream of tartar
50 g (2 oz) butter or hard margarine
150 ml (¼ pint) milk, plus extra for brushing
rind of 1 orange and ½ teaspoon orange juice
2 tablespoons demerara sugar

Preparation and cooking time: 45 minutes
Oven: 220°C, 425°F, Gas Mark 7

1. Arrange the apples in a 900 ml (1½ pint) ovenproof dish, sprinkle with the sugar and pour on the orange juice.
2. Stir in the dates and cover the fruit with the bananas tossed in the lemon juice.
3. To make the scone topping, sift together the flour, ginger, soda and cream of tartar and rub in the fat until the mixture is like crumbs.
4. Stir together the milk, orange rind and juice and pour on to the dry ingredients. Mix to a dough and knead it until it is smooth.
5. Roll the dough on a lightly floured board to a thickness of 1 cm (½ inch). Cut out rounds with a 5 cm (2 inch) cutter.
6. Arrange the scone rounds on the fruit, brush the tops with milk and sprinkle with the demerara sugar.
7. Bake the cobbler in a preheated oven for 20 minutes, or until the topping is well risen and golden brown. Serve hot.

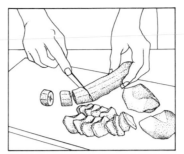

Prepare the cooking apples, put them into the dish and sprinkle with sugar and orange juice straightaway. Next peel and chop the banana. Toss the pieces in lemon juice to prevent browning

In a mixing bowl, sift in the dry ingredients for the scone topping and rub in the butter or margarine until the mixture resembles breadcrumbs. Pour in the liquids and mix to a dough in the bowl. Turn out on to a floured surface and knead until smooth

Roll out the dough on a floured surface using short forward strokes to a thickness of 1 cm (½ inch). Cut out rounds from the dough, using a 5 cm (2 inch) pastry cutter

Place the scone rounds on top of the fruit in the baking dish. Overlap them slightly and make sure the fruit is completely covered

HONEY CREAM

3 eggs, separated
3 tablespoons clear honey
200 ml (7 fl oz) double or whipping cream
2 tablespoons medium sherry
2 tablespoons chopped Brazil nuts

Preparation and cooking time: 45 minutes, including cooling

1. Whisk together the egg yolks and honey over a bowl of hot but not boiling water for about 5 minutes until the mixture is light and foamy. Remove the bowl from the pan, stand in a bowl of cold water and stir for 2 minutes.
2. Whip the cream until it is stiff and whisk the egg whites until they are stiff.
3. When the egg yolks are cool, stir in the cream and gradually stir in the sherry. Fold in the egg whites.
4. Divide the mixture between 4 individual glasses and sprinkle them with the nuts. Chill in the refrigerator before serving – just while you enjoy your main course will be long enough.

IN SIXTY MINUTES

BROWN RICE WITH CRISP VEGETABLES

1 medium onion, peeled and sliced
1 garlic clove, peeled and crushed
2 tablespoons olive oil
350 g (12 oz) brown long-grain rice
900 ml (1½ pint) chicken stock, hot
salt
freshly ground black pepper
1 small cauliflower, cut into small florets
225 g (8 oz) carrots, peeled and finely diced
2 leeks, peeled and sliced
100 g (4 oz) shelled peas
25 g (1 oz) butter
100 g (4 oz) Cheddar cheese, grated
1 tablespoon chopped mint
1 tablespoon chopped fresh parsley
grated Parmesan cheese, to serve

Preparation and cooking time: 1 hour

1. Fry the onion and garlic in the oil over moderate heat for 2 minutes, stirring once or twice. Stir in the rice and cook for 1 minute.
2. Pour on the hot stock, add salt and pepper, and bring to the boil. Cover the pan, lower the heat and simmer for 40 minutes. The rice should be just tender and have absorbed all the stock.
3. While the rice is cooking, steam the cauliflower, carrots, leeks and peas for about 10-12 minutes, until they are almost tender. It is very important that they retain their crispness.
4. Melt the butter in another pan and fry the vegetables, stirring frequently, for about 4 minutes, until they are glazed but not brown.
5. Stir the vegetables, Cheddar cheese and mint into the cooked rice. Garnish with the parsley and serve at once. Hand the Parmesan cheese separately.
6. For a perfect accompaniment, serve French bread slit through and spread with garlic butter, then foil-wrapped and crisped in a moderate oven for 15 minutes.

LENTIL AND WATERCRESS PATTIES

1 large onion, peeled and finely chopped
1 garlic clove, peeled and crushed
3 tablespoons vegetable oil
225 g (½ lb) split red lentils, washed and drained
600 ml (1 pint) chicken stock
few parsley stalks
2 tablespoons tomato purée
100 g (4 oz) blanched almonds, chopped
1 bunch watercress sprigs, finely chopped
1 tablespoon chopped mint
salt
freshly ground black pepper
2 tablespoons plain flour
oil for frying

Preparation and cooking time: 1 hour

1. Fry the onion and garlic in the oil over moderate heat for 2 minutes, stirring once or twice. Add the lentils and stir to coat them with oil.
2. Pour on the stock, add the parsley stalks and bring to the boil. Lower the heat, cover the pan and simmer for 40 minutes. The lentils should be soft and have absorbed the stock. If there is still some liquid increase the heat to evaporate it. Discard the parsley and remove the pan from the heat.
3. Beat the lentils with a wooden spoon and beat in the tomato purée, almonds, watercress and mint. Add salt and pepper.
4. Divide the mixture into 12 and mould into flat 'burger' shapes. Toss them in the flour to coat them thoroughly.
5. Fry the patties in hot oil over moderate heat for about 5 minutes on each side, or until they are crisp. Serve hot or cold.
6. These patties are very good, hot, with creamy mashed potatoes and a green vegetable. Served cold with salad, they make an unusual picnic snack.

Brown rice with crisp vegetables; Lentil and watercress patties

PRAWN MILLE FEUILLE

225 g (8 oz) bought puff pastry
Filling:
75 g (3 oz) butter
40 g (1½ oz) plain flour
300 ml (½ pint) milk
225 g (8 oz) shelled cooked prawns (thawed, if frozen)
1 teaspoon lemon juice
few drops of Tabasco sauce
salt
freshly ground black pepper
pinch of cayenne
150 ml (5 fl oz) double or whipping cream, thickly
  whipped
To garnish:
2 tablespoons canned concentrated consommé
2 tablespoons soured cream
4 button mushrooms, thinly sliced

**Preparation and cooking time: 1 hour, including
cooling**
Oven: 220°C, 425°F, Gas Mark 7

1. Divide the pastry into 3 equal pieces. Roll each
one to a rectangle about 13 × 25 cm (5 × 10 inches).
Rinse a baking sheet with cold water, arrange the
pastry and prick the tops all over with a fork.
2. Bake the pastry in a preheated oven for
12-15 minutes, until it is crisp and well browned.
Leave to cool.
3. Start to make the filling while the pastry is
cooking. Melt 40 kg (1½ oz) of the butter, stir in the
flour and then the milk. Bring to the boil, still stirring,
and simmer for 3 minutes. Remove from the heat,
stand the pan in a bowl of cold water and leave to
cool.
4. Beat the remaining butter until it is soft. Stir in the
prawns, reserving a few to garnish, and fold them into
the sauce which must be completely cool. Stir in the
lemon juice, Tabasco sauce and plenty of salt, pepper
and cayenne, and the cream.
5. Sandwich the pastry layers together with the
prawn filling.
6. Beat together the consommé and soured cream,
and add salt and pepper. Spread over the top of the
pastry and arrange the sliced mushrooms and
reserved prawns to garnish. Serve cold, with salad.
The mille feuille should only be sandwiched together
within 1 hour of serving in order that the pastry does
not go soft.

TANDOORI-STYLE CHICKEN

4 pieces of chicken, skinned
1 teaspoon salt
1 garlic clove, peeled and crushed
1 tablespoon tomato purée
1 tablespoon curry powder (mild or hot, to taste)
2 bay leaves, finely crumbled
juice of ½ lemon
450 ml (15 fl oz) plain unsweetened yogurt
75 g (3 oz) butter, melted
2 tablespoons paprika
1 lemon, quartered, to garnish

Preparation and cooking time: 1 hour
Oven: 200°C, 400°F, Gas Mark 6

1. Score the chicken flesh with a sharp knife. Place the chicken pieces in a casserole.
2. Mix together the salt, garlic, tomato purée, curry powder, bay leaves and lemon juice and stir in the yogurt. Pour this sauce over the chicken, then pour on the melted butter, leaving any foamy sediment behind. Cover the casserole and cook in a preheated oven for 50 minutes.
3. Pour off the sauce and keep it hot. Sprinkle the paprika over the chicken, rubbing it into the flesh, and return the dish, uncovered, to the oven for 5 minutes. Serve the sauce separately, garnished with lemon wedges.
4. Side dishes of raw green and red pepper rings and thin onion rings; banana slices dipped in lemon juice and rolled in desiccated coconut; and canned mandarin oranges add colour and interest.
5. If you have time to marinate the chicken pieces in the sauce, all day or overnight, the dish is even better. Pour on the melted butter just before you are ready to start cooking.

MATCHSTICKS OF BEEF IN RED WINE

100 g (4 oz) mushrooms, sliced
1 tablespoon vegetable oil
40 g (1½ oz) butter
1 medium onion, peeled and chopped
750 g (1½ lb) topside of beef, cut into matchstick strips
2 tablespoons plain flour
salt
freshly ground black pepper
½ teaspoon mixed dried herbs
1 garlic clove, peeled and crushed
1 tablespoon port
150 ml (¼ pint) beef stock
150 ml (¼ pint) red wine

Preparation and cooking time: 50 minutes

CHICKEN GOULASH

4 chicken breasts, skinned
salt
freshly ground black pepper
4 teaspoons paprika
2 tablespoons vegetable oil
2 medium onions, peeled and thinly sliced
2 green peppers, cored, seeded and sliced
3 tablespoons tomato purée
300 ml (10 fl oz) plain unsweetened yogurt
175 g (6 oz) mushrooms, sliced
sprigs of parsley, to garnish

Preparation and cooking time: 1 hour

1. Sprinkle the chicken with salt, pepper and 1 teaspoon of the paprika. Fry the chicken in the oil over moderate heat for 3 minutes on each side.
2. Remove the chicken and fry the onions and peppers, stirring once or twice, for 4 minutes. Stir in the remaining paprika and the tomato purée, then the yogurt.
3. Return the chicken to the pan, bring the sauce to the boil, cover and cook for 35 minutes, turning the chicken once during this time.
4. Add the mushrooms and continue cooking for 10 minutes. Taste the sauce and adjust the seasoning, if necessary. Garnish with the parsley sprigs.
5. Boiled rice or noodles are the perfect partner for the dish. If you choose noodles, try tossing them in plenty of butter with 1 teaspoon of caraway seeds for added flavour.

1. Fry the mushrooms in the oil and butter for 2 minutes over moderate heat, then remove. Fry the onion for 3-4 minutes, stirring once or twice.
2. Toss the beef strips in the flour mixed with salt, pepper and the dried herbs. Shake excess flour from the beef and add the meat to the pan. Fry for 5 minutes, stirring frequently.
3. Stir in the garlic, mushrooms, port, stock and wine and bring the sauce to the boil.
4. Reduce the heat to low, cover the pan and simmer for 25 minutes. Taste the sauce and adjust the seasoning, if necessary.
5. Serve with potatoes boiled in their skins, and a dish of mixed vegetables, such as peas and carrots.

CLOCKWISE FROM TOP LEFT: Tandoori-style chicken; Matchsticks of beef in red wine; Chicken goulash

HONEYED LAMB

750 g (1½ lb) lean lamb, cut from the leg
2 medium onions, peeled and sliced
2 medium carrots, peeled and sliced
2 sticks celery, thinly sliced
½ teaspoon dried thyme
120 ml (4 fl oz) sweet cider
2 tablespoons clear honey
1 tablespoon red wine vinegar
salt
freshly ground black pepper
7.5 g (¼ oz) butter
1 teaspoon flour

Preparation and cooking time: 1 hour
Oven: 200°C, 400°F, Gas Mark 6

1. Cut the meat into 1 inch cubes and trim off any fat. Put the onions, carrots and celery into a casserole and add the meat in a single layer. Sprinkle on the thyme.
2. Heat the cider and honey. When the honey has melted, stir in the vinegar and pour the sauce over the meat. Add salt and pepper.
3. Cover and cook in a preheated oven for 45 minutes.
4. Beat together the butter and flour, stir into the sauce and return to the oven for 5 minutes. Taste the sauce and adjust the seasoning.
5. Creamy puréed potatoes piped on to a dish and browned in the oven for 10 minutes make a delicious partner for this one-pot dish.

LAMB FRICASSÉE

750 g (1½ lb) lean lamb, cut from the leg
2 medium onions, peeled and thinly sliced
1 garlic clove, peeled and crushed
40 g (1½ oz) butter
1 tablespoon vegetable oil
2 lemons
1 tablespoon plain flour
300 ml (½ pint) chicken stock, hot
salt
freshly ground black pepper
3 egg yolks
1 tablespoon chopped fresh parsley

Preparation and cooking time: 1 hour

1. Cut the meat into 2.5 cm (1 inch) cubes and trim off any fat.
2. Fry the onions and garlic in the butter and oil for 3-4 minutes over moderate heat, then temporarily remove them with a draining spoon.
3. Slightly increase the heat and fry the cubes of meat to brown them on all sides. Lower the heat to moderate again. Stir in the grated rind of 1 lemon and the flour and cook for 1 minute.
4. Pour on the hot stock, add salt and pepper, return the onions and garlic and bring to the boil. Cover and simmer for 45 minutes.
5. Beat the egg yolks with 3 tablespoons lemon juice and stir in 4 tablespoons of the stock mixture. Lower the heat, pour the egg mixture on to the meat, stir well and stir for about 4 minutes. Do not allow it to boil. Taste the seasoning and adjust, if necessary.
6. Garnish with the parsley. Serve hot.
7. Accompany with broccoli, cauliflower or Brussels sprouts and new potatoes or pasta shapes.

PORK CHOPS IN NORMANDY SAUCE

4 loin of pork chops
25 g (1 oz) butter
1 tablespoon oil
2 medium onions, peeled and sliced
1 garlic clove, peeled and crushed
2 medium cooking apples, peeled, cored and thickly sliced
½ teaspoon dried thyme
250 ml (8 fl oz) sweet cider
1 tablespoon clear honey
1 tablespoon brandy (optional)
salt
freshly ground black pepper
4 tablespoons double cream

Preparation and cooking time: 1 hour
Oven: 190°C, 375°F, Gas Mark 5

1. Trim the excess fat from the chops. Fry them in half the butter and the oil over moderately high heat for 3 minutes on each side. Transfer to a casserole.
2. Add the remaining butter and fry the onions and garlic over moderate heat for 3 minutes. Transfer them to the casserole.
3. Fry the apple slices for 1 minute on each side and add them to the casserole.
4. Add the thyme, pour on the cider, add the honey, brandy, if used and salt and pepper. Stir the sauce, cover and cook in a preheated oven for 35 minutes.
5. Skim off the fat that has risen to the surface and stir in the cream. Taste and adjust the seasoning and sweetness, if necessary. Serve hot.
6. This pork and cream dish is very rich and is best with a selection of fresh vegetables, such as tiny carrots, whole French beans and peas, tossed in plenty of chopped mint and ground black pepper.

MEATBALLS IN HORSERADISH SAUCE

1 × 1 cm (½ inch) thick slice of white bread cut from a
 large loaf, crusts removed
450 g (1 lb) lean beef, minced twice
salt
freshly ground black pepper
¼ teaspoon mustard powder
1 egg, beaten
40 g (1½ oz) butter
1 tablespoon chopped fresh parsley, to garnish
Sauce:
2 teaspoons plain flour
300 ml (½ pint) chicken stock
2 tablespoons horseradish sauce
½ teaspoon lemon juice

Preparation and cooking time: 50 minutes

Lamb fricassée; Meatballs in horseradish sauce

1. Soak the bread for a few minutes in water, then
squeeze it dry.
2. Mix together the bread and minced meat, mashing
it vigorously with a wooden spoon until it forms a
paste. Add salt, pepper and mustard powder and beat
in the egg. If you have a food processor, put in all the
ingredients and switch on for a few seconds.
3. Flour your hands and shape the meat into balls
about the size of a table tennis ball. Fry them in 25 g
(1 oz) of the butter, turning them over and over until
they are evenly brown and crisp – about 6-8 minutes.
Remove the meatballs from the pan.
4. Melt the remaining butter in the pan, stir in the
flour and then the stock. Bring to the boil, stir in the
horseradish sauce and lemon juice, and add salt and
pepper to taste.
5. Return the meatballs to the pan, cover and simmer
over low heat for 3 minutes. Taste and adjust the
seasoning, if necessary.
6. Garnish with the parsley and serve hot.

STEAMED LEMON AND RAISIN PUDDINGS

100 g (4 oz) self-raising flour
1 teaspoon baking powder
100 g (4 oz) caster sugar
100 g (4 oz) soft margarine
2 large eggs
grated rind of 2 lemons
3 tablespoons lemon juice
100 g (4 oz) seedless raisins
Sauce:
4 tablespoons clear honey
1 tablespoon rum or brandy (optional)
grated rind of 2 lemons
4 tablespoons lemon juice
2 tablespoons water
3 tablespoons raisins

Preparation and cooking time: 1 hour

1. Sift the flour and baking powder. Beat in the sugar, soft margarine, eggs, lemon rind and lemon juice and beat until the mixture is smooth. Stir in the raisins.
2. Spoon the mixture into 8 greased ramekin dishes or small dariole moulds and cover the tops with greased foil. Place in a large frying pan or saucepan with boiling water to come halfway up the dishes. Bring quickly back to the boil, cover and cook for 45 minutes, keeping the water at a boil. Top up with more boiling water as needed.
3. Make the sauce while the puddings are cooking. Put all the ingredients into a small pan and heat them gently, so that the raisins absorb the honey and lemon flavour. Serve the sauce warm.
4. Run a knife all round between the puddings and the moulds and turn them out on to a warmed flat serving plate. Spoon a little of the sauce over to glaze and decorate the puddings, and serve the remaining sauce separately.

ORANGE BREAD AND BUTTER PUDDING

6 thin slices of wholemeal or white bread, crusts removed
50 g (2 oz) butter
rind of 2 oranges
50 g (2 oz) raisins
40 g (1½ oz) sugar
¼ teaspoon ground cinnamon
a few drops of vanilla essence
600 ml (1 pint) milk
2 eggs, separated
To decorate:
1 orange, thinly sliced
1 tablespoon redcurrant jelly

Preparation and cooking time: 50 minutes
Oven: 190°C, 375°F, Gas Mark 5

1. Spread the bread with butter and cut each slice into 4 triangles. Arrange the slices to cover a greased 1 litre (2 pint) baking dish, sprinkling the grated orange rind and raisins between them.
2. Stir the sugar, cinnamon and vanilla into the milk and beat in the egg yolks. Stiffly whisk the egg whites and fold them into the milk mixture. Pour over the bread.
3. Bake in a preheated oven for 40-45 minutes, until the pudding is well risen and golden brown.
4. Meanwhile blanch the orange slices in a little boiling water for about 5 minutes.
5. Arrange the orange slices on top to decorate the pudding. Brush the jelly over the orange slices to glaze them. Serve the pudding hot, with chilled whipped cream.

Orange bread and butter pudding; Steamed lemon and raisin pudding; American pancake gâteau

AMERICAN PANCAKE GATEAU

225 g (8 oz) plain flour
2 teaspoons baking powder
1 tablespoon caster sugar
½ teaspoon ground cinnamon
1 teaspoon salt
2 large eggs
450 ml (¾ pint) milk
4 tablespoons melted butter
25 g (1 oz) butter, for frying
Sauce:
450 g (1 lb) fresh cherries, pitted
300 ml (½ pint) red grape juice
1 tablespoon lemon juice
2 tablespoons clear honey
4 teaspoons arrowroot

Preparation and cooking time: 1 hour

Instead of fresh cherries, you could use 1 × 400 g (15 oz) can of pitted cherries. Make up the syrup to 300 ml (½ pint) with water. There will be fewer cherries in the sauce, but it will still be very good.
1. Begin by making the sauce. Place the cherries, grape juice, lemon juice and honey in a pan and bring slowly to the boil. Simmer for 10 minutes, or until the fruit is soft. Strain the cherries from the juice and set them aside.
2. Measure the juice and make it up to 300 ml (½ pint) with water. Mix a little of the juice into the arrowroot and stir to make a smooth paste. Pour on the remaining juice, return to the pan and stir over moderate heat until the sauce boils. Stir for 2 minutes, until the sauce clears and thickens.
3. Return the cherries to the sauce, cover the top with wetted greaseproof paper and keep warm.
4. To make the pancakes, sift together the flour, baking powder, sugar, cinnamon and salt. Beat in the eggs one at a time, then gradually beat in the milk. Pour on the melted butter and beat well. Or blend all the ingredients for a few seconds in a blender.
5. Heat a small frying pan or an omelette pan and grease it with some of the butter. Pour 3 tablespoons of the mixture into the pan and cook the pancake over high heat for 2-3 minutes, until the surface bubbles. Flip the pancake over and cook the other side for 2 minutes, or until it is equally brown.
6. Keep the cooked pancake warm on a covered plate over a pan of hot water while you make the remainder. Grease the pan with more butter as necessary. The mixture should make 16 small pancakes.
7. Gently reheat the sauce. Put one pancake on each of 4 individual plates. Spoon a little of the sauce between each and pile up 4 pancakes on each plate. Serve the remainder of the sauce separately.
8. Serve the pancakes hot, with single cream.

AHEAD OF TIME

BRAISED VEAL WITH ARTICHOKE HEARTS

4 fillets of veal, about 100 g (4 oz) each
75 g (3 oz) butter
1 small onion, peeled and thinly sliced
1 garlic clove, peeled and crushed
50 g (2 oz) button mushrooms, sliced
1 teaspoon dried rosemary, crumbled
200 ml (⅓ pint) white wine or dry cider
1 × 400 g (14 oz) can artichoke hearts, drained and halved
salt
freshly ground black pepper
1 teaspoon plain flour
4 tablespoons double cream

Preparation time: 10 minutes
Cooking time: 50 minutes
Oven: 160°C, 325°F, Gas Mark 3

1. Cut each veal fillet into 3 pieces. Fry in 25 g (1 oz) of the butter over moderate heat for 2 minutes on each side. Transfer the veal to a flameproof casserole.
2. Fry the onion in 25 g (1 oz) butter for 2 minutes. Add the garlic and mushrooms, stir well and fry for a further 2 minutes. Transfer to the casserole.
3. Add the rosemary, wine or cider and artichoke hearts to the pan, bring to the boil, and add salt and pepper. Pour into the casserole and cook in a preheated oven for 30 minutes.
4. Beat together the flour and the remaining butter. Remove the casserole from the oven, stir the paste into the liquor and bring to the boil on top of the cooker. Simmer for 2-3 minutes, until the sauce has thickened.
5. Stir in the cream and allow to heat, without boiling. Taste and adjust the seasoning, if necessary.
6. New potatoes and spinach make a good accompaniment.

Beforehand:
Cook the casserole to the end of step 3, then cool and store for up to 2 days in the refrigerator.

On the day:
Reheat the casserole at 160°C, 325°F, Gas Mark 3 for 25-30 minutes. Then stir in the butter paste and cream as described in steps 4 and 5.

PORK AND APRICOT CASSEROLE

750 g (1¾ lb) lean leg of pork
2 tablespoons plain flour
salt
freshly ground black pepper
1 teaspoon dried thyme
4 tablespoons olive oil
2 medium onions, peeled and sliced
1 garlic clove, peeled and crushed
4 tender celery sticks, thinly sliced
300 ml (½ pint) chicken stock
225 g (8 oz) dried apricots, soaked overnight in 300 ml (½ pint) orange juice
2 teaspoons chopped fresh parsley, to garnish

Preparation time: 15 minutes, plus overnight soaking
Cooking time: 1 hour
Oven: 180°C, 350°F, Gas Mark 4

1. Trim the pork and cut it into 2.5 cm × 1 cm (1 inch × ½ inch) slices. Toss them in the flour mixed with salt, pepper and dried thyme.
2. Fry the pork slices in the oil in a pan over moderately high heat for about 8 minutes, turning them to brown evenly. Transfer the meat to a casserole, lower the heat to moderate and fry the onions, garlic and celery in the oil, stirring occasionally, for 4 minutes. Transfer the vegetables to the casserole.
3. Stir the chicken stock into the pan, add the apricots and the soaking liquid and bring to the boil.
4. Pour the sauce over the meat, taste and adjust seasoning, if necessary. Cook in a preheated oven for 45 minutes, until the pork and vegetables are tender.
5. Garnish with the parsley.
6. Rice and a green vegetable such as green beans or broccoli spears are ideal with this colourful dish.

Beforehand:
Cook the casserole, cool and store in the refrigerator for up to 24 hours.

On the day:
Reheat the casserole at 160°C, 325°F, Gas Mark 3 for 30 minutes, then sprinkle on the parsley.

Pork and apricot casserole

CHILLED AUBERGINES

4 medium aubergines
salt
225 g (8 oz) sausagemeat
1 small onion, grated or finely chopped
2 tablespoons sultanas
2 large tomatoes, skinned and chopped
½ teaspoon ground coriander
2 tablespoons chopped fresh parsley
freshly ground black pepper
6 tablespoons olive oil
4 tablespoons chicken stock or water

Preparation time: 45 minutes, plus chilling
Cooking time: 45-50 minutes
Oven: 180°C, 350°F, Gas Mark 4

1. Halve the aubergines lengthways. Using a teaspoon or vegetable baller, scoop out the flesh, leaving 'walls' about 5 mm (¼ inch) thick. Put the aubergine flesh in a colander and sprinkle it with salt. Sprinkle salt on to the cut sides of the aubergine halves and put them cut sides down in the colander. Leave to drain for 30 minutes, while you make the filling.
2. Mash the sausagemeat in a bowl and stir in the onion, sultanas, tomatoes, coriander, half the parsley, and salt and pepper.
3. Rinse the aubergines and pat dry with kitchen towels. Chop the aubergine flesh and stir it into the meat mixture. Pile into the shells and pack down firmly.
4. Arrange the aubergines in a single layer in a shallow baking dish and pour the oil and stock or water round them. Cook uncovered in a preheated oven for 45-50 minutes.
5. Leave the aubergines in the dish to cool. Cover and chill in the refrigerator. Garnish with the reserved parsley.
6. This dish makes a substantial and interesting first course. It could also be served hot as a main course with boiled potatoes and a green vegetable or salad.

Beforehand:
Prepare and cook a day in advance.

On the day:
Transfer the aubergines to a clean serving dish, spoon the sauce round them and garnish with parsley.

POTTED BACON

275 g (10 oz) lean cooked bacon (e.g. hock or collar), rinded
100 g (4 oz) unsalted butter, melted and cooled
4 tablespoons double cream
1 tablespoon chopped fresh parsley
1 teaspoon prepared English mustard
2 tablespoons dry sherry
pinch of ground nutmeg
freshly ground black pepper
1 red pepper, to garnish
8 slices of bread

Preparation time: 20 minutes, plus chilling

1. Trim excess fat from the bacon. Mince it to coarse or fine consistency, as you prefer.
2. Stir three-quarters of the butter into the bacon and mix well. Stir in the cream, parsley, mustard and sherry, and add nutmeg and pepper, to taste.
3. Turn the mixture into a straight-sided serving dish (such as a small casserole) and pack it down firmly, using the back of a spoon.
4. Pour on the remaining butter (it may be necessary to melt it again) and tip the dish to spread the butter in a thin film.
5. Cover the dish with foil or cling-film and leave it in the refrigerator to chill for at least 1 hour.
6. Quarter the red pepper, discard the seeds and stalk and cut the flesh into small diamond or leaf shapes to garnish the top of the dish.
7. Toast the bread, cut into triangles and serve hot.
8. Potted bacon can be served as a first course, or as a light lunch or supper dish, with salad.

Beforehand:
Make the potted bacon and store it, covered, in the refrigerator for up to 4 days.
  Cut the pepper shapes for the garnish and store them in a small covered container for 1-2 days.

On the day:
Arrange the garnish on the dish. Make the toast.

CLOCKWISE FROM BOTTOM LEFT: Chilled aubergines; Potted bacon; Blue cheese mousse

BLUE CHEESE MOUSSE

15 g (½ oz) powdered gelatine
3 tablespoons hot water
2 eggs, separated
1 tablespoon Worcestershire sauce
75 g (3 oz) chopped walnuts
100 g (4 oz) Danish blue or Roquefort cheese, crumbled
300 ml (10 fl oz) double or whipping cream, whipped

To garnish:
8 walnut halves
1 bunch watercress, trimmed and divided into sprigs
1 small cucumber, thinly sliced

Preparation time: 30 minutes, plus chilling

1. Dissolve the gelatine in the water and leave to cool.
2. Beat the egg yolks until creamy. Whisk the whites until stiff.
3. Stir the egg yolks, Worcestershire sauce and walnuts into the cheese. When the gelatine is cool, pour it slowly into the mixture, stirring to mix well.
4. Fold in the whipped cream, then the egg whites.
5. Rinse a 900 ml (1½ pint) mould or bowl in cold water and pour in the cheese mixture. Leave in the refrigerator for at least 2 hours to set and chill.
6. Unmould the mousse on to a serving plate. Garnish the top with the walnut halves and a few sprigs of watercress. Arrange the cucumber slices and remaining watercress round the base.

Beforehand:
Make the mousse and store it (also the sliced cucumber in a covered container) in the refrigerator for up to 24 hours.

On the day:
Turn out the mould and arrange the garnish.

HADDOCK CASSEROLE WITH GARLIC SAUCE

750 g (1½ lb) fresh haddock fillets
2 large onions, peeled and sliced
2 garlic cloves, peeled and crushed
3 tablespoons olive oil
1 × 400 g (14 oz) can tomatoes
1 tablespoon chopped fresh parsley
1 tablespoon chopped fresh mint
150 ml (¼ pint) water
300 ml (½ pint) dry cider
2 bay leaves
a few parsley stalks
10-13 cm (4-5 inch) strip thinly pared orange rind
450 g (1 lb) potatoes, peeled and diced
salt
freshly ground black pepper
Sauce:
4 tablespoons mayonnaise
2 garlic cloves, peeled and crushed
1 tablespoon tomato purée
1 tablespoon chopped fresh mint

Preparation time: 20 minutes
Cooking time: 55 minutes

1. Trim and skin the fish and cut it into 7.5 cm (3 inch) slices.
2. Fry the onions and garlic in the oil in a flameproof casserole over low heat for 8-10 minutes, stirring occasionally. Add the tomatoes, parsley and mint, increase the heat to moderate and cook for 10 minutes.
3. Add the water, cider, bay leaves, parsley stalks and orange rind. Bring back to the boil.
4. Add the potatoes, salt and pepper, cover the casserole and simmer for 20 minutes. Add the fish and simmer for 12-15 minutes, until it is just firm. Discard the bay leaves, parsley and orange rind. Taste and adjust seasoning, if necessary.
5. To make the sauce, stir the ingredients together until they are well blended. Serve separately, to be spooned on top of the fish.

Beforehand:
The dish is greatly improved by being cooked in advance. Cool, then store in a covered container in the refrigerator for up to 24 hours.
   You can make the sauce up to 3 days in advance.

On the day:
Reheat the casserole over a low heat for about 15 minutes. Bring it just to the boil.

SOUSED HERRINGS

4 large herrings
150 ml (¼ pint) water
150 ml (¼ pint) red wine vinegar
6-8 black or green peppercorns
2 bay leaves
1 small onion, peeled and sliced into rings
2 small gherkins, thinly sliced
1 red pepper, cored, seeded and thinly sliced
1 orange, thinly sliced, to garnish

Preparation time: 15 minutes, plus cooling and setting
Cooking time: 40-45 minutes
Oven: 180°C, 350°F, Gas Mark 4

Haddock casserole with garlic sauce; Soused herrings

1. Cut the heads from the herrings. Clean and gut the fish and scrape off the scales. Remove the backbone and slit them in half. Wash the fillets. Roll up the fillets, skin side out. Secure with wooden cocktail sticks.
2. Arrange the fillets in a shallow ovenproof dish, pour on the water and vinegar, and add the remaining ingredients.
3. Cover the dish with foil and cook in a preheated oven for 40-45 minutes.
4. Remove from the oven and leave the fillets to cool in the liquid. Once cold, you can store them in the refrigerator for up to 3 days.
5. Transfer the fillets to a serving dish, discarding the liquid, peppercorns, and bay leaves. Garnish them with the onion, gherkins and red pepper and then with the orange slices.
6. Serve with plenty of crusty wholemeal bread.

Beforehand:
Here's a dish that *has* to be cooked in advance so that the herring fillets have time to cool. Follow the recipe to the end of step 4.

On the day:
Continue with step 5 of the recipe – 3 minutes at the most!

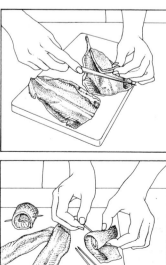

Cut off the heads. Then, using the blunt side of a knife and scraping from the tail towards the head, remove the scales. Rinse in cold water. With a sharp knife, make a slit along the belly from the top to the tail and clean out the entrails

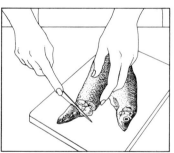

Open out the fish on the chopping board, cut side down and press firmly along the backbone. Turn the fish over and remove the loosened backbone with a knife, starting at the head

Wash in cold water, cut off the tails, then slit the fillets in half lengthways. Roll up each piece, skin side out and push a wooden cocktail stick through the middle to secure

CORIANDER LAMB WITH ORANGE RICE

3 large onions, peeled and grated or minced
2 bay leaves, very finely crumbled
100 g (4 oz) butter
6 tablespoons water
750 g (1½ lb) lean lamb, cut into 2.5 cm (1 inch) cubes
2 garlic cloves, peeled and crushed
1 cm (½ inch) piece fresh ginger, peeled and finely
    chopped
1 tablespoon ground coriander
1 teaspoon ground cumin
2 teaspoons paprika
½ teaspoon cayenne (or to taste)
1 teaspoon salt
150 ml (5 fl oz) plain unsweetened yogurt
225 g (½ lb) potatoes, peeled and diced
2 teaspoons lemon juice
4 large tomatoes, skinned and quartered
1 lemon, quartered, to serve
Orange rice:
1 tablespoon vegetable oil
225 g (8 oz) long-grain rice
1 teaspoon ground turmeric
600 ml (1 pint) chicken stock, or water
1 teaspoon salt
1 orange
2 tablespoons blanched almonds, toasted
1 tablespoon chopped fresh parsley

Preparation time: 30 minutes
Cooking time: 1¾ hours
Oven: 180°C, 350°F, Gas Mark 4

1. Fry the onions and bay leaves in half the butter over moderate heat for 8-10 minutes, stirring frequently until they are medium brown, but not burning. Stir in 1 tablespoon of the water until it forms a paste. Transfer the onions to a casserole.
2. Fry the lamb in the remaining butter for about 3 minutes on each side, until it is sealed. Transfer the meat to the casserole.
3. Fry the garlic and ginger in the fat remaining in the pan for 2 minutes, then stir in the spices and cook for 1 minute. Stir in the remaining water, salt and yogurt, and bring the sauce slowly to the boil.
4. Cover the casserole and cook in a preheated oven for 30 minutes. Add the potatoes and lemon juice and cook for a further 45 minutes.
5. Add the sliced tomatoes and cook for a further 5 minutes. Serve with the lemon wedges.
6. About 30 minutes before the lamb dish is ready, start cooking the orange rice. Heat the vegetable oil in a pan and stir the rice over moderate heat for 1 minute. Stir in the turmeric, then add the stock or water, and the salt. Cover the pan and simmer for 20 minutes, or until the rice is just tender.

7. Meanwhile, grate the orange rind. Peel the orange and divide the flesh into segments.
8. Remove the pan from the heat and leave the rice to rest for 5 minutes before serving. Stir in the orange rind and segments and most of the almonds. Garnish the rice with a few almonds and the parsley.

Beforehand:
Cook the casserole to the end of step 4, then cool. Store it in the refrigerator for 1-2 days. Toast the almonds and prepare the orange for the rice.

On the day:
Reheat the casserole in a preheated oven at 160°C, 325°F, Gas Mark 3 for 30 minutes. Complete steps 5-8.

PORK FILLET IN CURRY SAUCE

2 pork fillets, about 750 g (1½ lb) together
300 ml (10 fl oz) plain unsweetened yogurt
2 teaspoons curry powder (mild or hot, to taste)
1 teaspoon ground turmeric
1 teaspoon salt
½ teaspoon freshly ground black pepper
½ teaspoon paprika
1 medium onion, peeled and finely chopped
2 garlic cloves, peeled and crushed
50 g (2 oz) butter
3 tablespoons ground almonds
300 ml (½ pint) boiling water
75-150 g (3-5 oz) desiccated coconut
To garnish:
1 large lemon, thinly sliced
2 large, firm tomatoes, thinly sliced

Preparation time: 25 minutes, plus marinating
Cooking time: 1 hour 50 minutes

1. Trim the pork fillets, cutting off the pointed ends to make a neat shape.
2. Stir the yogurt with the curry powder, turmeric, salt, pepper and paprika. Pour the mixture over the pork and turn the meat to coat it thoroughly with the marinade. Cover and chill for 1 hour.
3. Fry the onion and garlic in the butter over moderate heat for 4 minutes, stirring once or twice.
4. Add the pork and the yogurt marinade, bring to simmering point and simmer for 5 minutes. Stir in the ground almonds and barely simmer over very low heat (using an asbestos mat if necessary) for 1½ hours, turning the meat in the sauce occasionally.
5. Pour the boiling water over the coconut and leave to soak for 10 minutes. Line a sieve with muslin, or using a very finely woven nylon sieve, tip in the coconut and liquid and press with a wooden spoon to extract all the moisture.
6. Add the coconut liquid to the meat, stir the sauce and simmer for a further 10 minutes. Taste the sauce and adjust the seasoning, if necessary.
7. To serve the meat, cut deep slits in the pork fillets, about 3 cm (1¼ inches) apart. Cut the lemon slices in halves. Arrange slices of lemon and tomato alternately in the slits.
8. The sauce in this dish is, characteristically, very liquid. You can thicken it by simmering for longer or by stirring in a little of the soaked coconut.
9. Prepare plenty of rice to accompany the dish and soak up the sauce. Offer a variety of mild and hot savouries – mango or peach chutney, home-made tomato or apple chutney and hot lime pickle all add interest. Poppadoms and chappatis (or pitta bread) are almost a 'must'. Then have 'instant' side dishes of desiccated coconut, sultanas, toasted almonds and sliced banana to add to the curry.

Beforehand:
Prepare the dish to the end of step 5. Assemble the jars of chutney, sultanas and so on, to avoid searching the kitchen cupboards at the last minute.

On the day:
Reheat the dish on top of the cooker. Garnish the meat with the lemon and tomato slices. Cook the rice. Grill or fry the poppadoms. Heat the chappatis or pitta. Place the chutneys, coconut, sultanas, etc. in bowls.

Coriander lamb with orange rice; Pork fillet in curry sauce

LAMB CUTLETS IN ASPIC

2 pieces of best end of neck of lamb, 8 cutlets in total
salt
freshly ground black pepper
40 g (1½ oz) aspic crystals
175 ml (6 fl oz) condensed consommé, hot
5 tablespoons dry sherry
To garnish:
1 cooked carrot, thinly sliced
strips of cucumber
lettuce leaves
sprigs of mint

Preparation time: 25 minutes, plus cooling and setting
Cooking time: 35 minutes
Oven: 160°C, 325°F, Gas Mark 3

1. Trim the skin and any excess fat from the lamb and cut the meat away to expose 2.5 cm (1 inch) of the bone. Sprinkle with salt and pepper.
2. Cook the lamb for about 35 minutes in a preheated oven, turning once during cooking. Cool on a rack for about 40 minutes.
3. Dissolve the aspic in the hot stock, stir in the sherry and add pepper to taste.
4. Cut the lamb into separate cutlets and place on a wire rack over a tray.
5. Cut flower shapes from the carrot slices, using an aspic cutter. Arrange the 'flowers' on the lamb and use the strips of cucumber for stalks and tiny leaves.
6. When the aspic is syrupy, spoon it over the lamb to coat the top and sides. Chill the lamb for about 1 hour in the refrigerator to allow the aspic to set. Arrange it on a bed of lettuce and garnish with sprigs of mint.
7. Tiny new potatoes and peas are perfect with this impressive-looking dish.

Beforehand:
Cook, chill and coat the lamb a day in advance. Even before that, you can cut the carrots for garnish and store in the refrigerator.

On the day:
Serve with style!

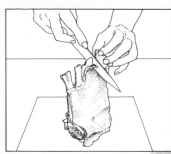
Cut away the meat to expose the bones

Cut between each bone to separate the meat into cutlets

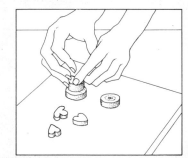
Cut 3 shapes per cutlet from the carrot

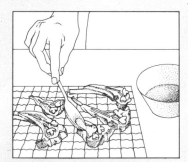
Place the cutlets on a wire tray and spoon over the aspic syrup

LAMB CHOPS IN RED WINE SAUCE

4 large loin of lamb chops or 8 small ones
1 garlic clove, peeled and finely chopped
2 small courgettes, trimmed and sliced
175 g (6 oz) button mushrooms, sliced
25 g (1 oz) butter
4 large tomatoes, skinned and sliced
1 tablespoon clear honey
150 ml (¼ pint) red wine
1 tablespoon chopped fresh marjoram or 1 teaspoon dried
  marjoram
salt
freshly ground black pepper
1 tablespoon chopped fresh parsley, to garnish

Preparation time: 20 minutes
Cooking time: 35 minutes
Oven: 190°C, 375°F, Gas Mark 5

1. Trim excess fat from the chops. Fry them with the garlic in a non-stick frying pan over moderate heat for 3 minutes on each side. Transfer the chops to a casserole. Discard any fat remaining in the pan.
2. Fry the courgettes and mushrooms in the butter, stirring them once or twice, for 2 minutes. Add them to the chops.
3. Add the tomatoes, honey, wine, marjoram, salt and pepper.
4. Cover the casserole and cook in a preheated oven for 25 minutes.
5. Serve garnished with parsley. As a cool, crisp contrast, prepare a salad of sliced green peppers, diced cucumber and sliced cabbage. Toss in French dressing just before serving.
6. Wholewheat pasta tossed with butter and chopped parsley makes a lovely accompaniment, and is very quick to cook at the last minute.

Beforehand:
Cook the casserole, cool, then store in the refrigerator for 1-2 days. Store the salad overnight in a covered box in the refrigerator.

On the day:
Reheat the casserole for about 30 minutes at 180°C, 350°F, Gas Mark 4. Taste the sauce and adjust the seasoning if necessary. Garnish.

COURGETTE MOUSSAKA

750 g (1½ lb) courgettes, trimmed and thinly sliced
8 tablespoons olive oil
1 large onion, peeled and thinly sliced
2 green peppers, trimmed, seeded and sliced
1 garlic clove, peeled and crushed
450 g (1 lb) tomatoes, skinned and sliced
1 tablespoon tomato purée
1 tablespoon chopped fresh mint
salt
freshly ground black pepper
100 g (4 oz) Gruyère cheese, thinly sliced
2 tablespoons plain flour
300 ml (10 fl oz) plain unsweetened yogurt
2 egg yolks
75 g (3 oz) Cheddar cheese, grated

Preparation time: 20 minutes
Cooking time: 50 minutes
Oven: 200°C, 400°F, Gas Mark 6

1. Fry the courgette slices a few at a time in the oil over moderate heat. Turn them to brown evenly on both sides. Set aside while you fry the remainder.
2. Fry the onion, peppers and garlic in the pan for about 4 minutes, stirring once or twice. Add a little more oil if necessary.
3. Stir in the tomatoes, tomato purée, mint, salt and pepper. Cook for a further 2 minutes.
4. Arrange a layer of courgettes in a greased shallow baking dish. Cover with half the tomato mixture, then with the sliced cheese. Make a layer of the remaining tomato mixture, and cover with the remaining courgette slices.
5. Mix together the flour, yogurt, egg yolks, grated cheese, salt and pepper. Pour over the courgettes.
6. Stand the dish on a baking sheet and cook, uncovered, in a preheated oven for 25 minutes, until the top is deep brown. Serve hot.
7. Both pasta and potatoes are delicious with this colourful vegetable dish – take your choice!

Beforehand:
Assemble the dish ready to cook up to and including step 4, cover with film or foil and store in the refrigerator for up to 24 hours. You *can* cook it in advance, but it will take 20 minutes to heat through in a preheated oven at 190°C, 375°F, Gas Mark 5.

On the day:
Proceed with step 5.

Lamb chops in red wine sauce; Courgette moussaka

CLOCKWISE FROM BOTTOM LEFT: Honeycomb mould; Ginger biscuit cream cake; Rosewater sponge drops

HONEYCOMB MOULD

600 ml (1 pint) single cream
2 eggs, separated
2 tablespoons clear honey
¼ teaspoon vanilla essence
15 g (½ oz) powdered gelatine
2 tablespoons warm water
450 g (1 lb) mixed soft fruits
fruit leaves, to decorate

Preparation time: 5 minutes, plus setting
Cooking time: 30 minutes

1. Heat the cream slowly until it is just below boiling point.
2. Beat together the egg yolks and honey, until they are pale and foamy. Gradually pour on the heated cream, still beating.
3. Pour the mixture into a pan over very low heat, or the top of a double boiler over a little simmering water. Stir until the mixture thickens enough to coat the back of a spoon. Stir in the vanilla essence.

4. Dissolve the gelatine in the water and pour it slowly into the custard mixture, stirring all the time. Leave the mixture in a bowl of iced water to cool.
5. Whisk the egg whites until stiff and fold into the mixture when it is syrupy and on the point of setting.
6. Rinse a 900 ml (1½ pint) mould or bowl with cold water. Pour in the honey mixture and level the top. Refrigerate for at least 2 hours before turning out.
7. Run a knife between the mould and the dessert. Hold a serving dish over the rim, give a sharp shake and turn out the mould. Surround the mould with the soft fruits to serve. Decorate with a few blackberry, raspberry, strawberry or vine leaves.

Beforehand:
Make the mould and refrigerate for up to 24 hours before serving. Hull the fruits, or thaw frozen ones, and keep them chilled in a covered container.

On the day:
Turn out the mould, arrange the fruits around it and decorate.

GINGER BISCUIT CREAM CAKE

300 ml (10 fl oz) double or whipping cream
1 tablespoon sweet sherry (optional)
3 tablespoons mixed candied peel, finely chopped
175 g (6 oz) ginger biscuits
fresh strawberries, to decorate

Preparation time: 15 minutes, plus chilling

1. Whip the cream until thick and stir in the sherry if used and the chopped peel.
2. Sandwich all the biscuits together to form a roll, using about half the cream mixture.
3. Place the biscuit roll on a serving plate, then spread on the remaining cream to cover it.
4. Cover the cake loosely with foil and chill in the refrigerator for at least 5-6 hours. During this time the biscuits will soften and all the flavours blend.
5. Cut each strawberry into slices. Decorate the cake with a row of the sliced strawberries along the centre.

Beforehand:
Make and chill the cake. It stores well in the refrigerator for up to 2 days.

On the day:
Nothing to do but serve!

ORANGE AND NUT PASHKA

225 g (8 oz) cottage cheese, sieved
150 ml (5 fl oz) soured cream
75 g (3 oz) caster sugar
grated rind of 1 orange
100 g (4 oz) blanched almonds, toasted
4 tablespoons orange-flavoured liqueur
4 oranges, peeled and thinly sliced

Preparation time: 15 minutes, plus standing

1. Beat together the cottage cheese, soured cream, half the sugar, the orange rind and almonds.
2. Place a sieve over a bowl, line it with muslin or cheesecloth, or use a very finely woven nylon sieve, and spoon the cheese mixture into it. Place a small saucer on the cheese, with a weight on top to press it down. Leave overnight or for up to 24 hours.

ROSEWATER SPONGE DROPS

Makes 6 pairs
2 large eggs
100 g (4 oz) caster sugar
100 g (4 oz) plain flour
1 teaspoon baking powder
2 teaspoons triple strength rosewater from chemists
caster sugar, for dredging
Filling:
150 ml (5 fl oz) double or whipping cream, whipped
a few drops of triple strength rosewater
2-3 drops of pink edible food colouring

Preparation time: 35 minutes, plus cooling
Cooking time: 10 minutes
Oven: 190°C, 375°F, Gas Mark 5

1. Beat together the eggs and sugar until the mixture is thick and foamy.
2. Sift the flour and baking powder. Fold it into the egg mixture, a little at a time. Stir in the rosewater.
3. Drop teaspoons of the mixture on to 2 greased baking sheets. Bake in a preheated oven for 10 minutes.
4. Transfer the sponge drops to a wire tray to cool. Leave for at least 30 minutes before filling them.
5. Stir the rosewater and colouring into the whipped cream. Sandwich the sponge drops together in pairs with the cream. Dust the tops with caster sugar.

Beforehand:
Make the sponge drops and store in an airtight tin. Make the filling and refrigerate for up to 24 hours.

On the day:
Sandwich together and dust with sugar.

3. Turn out the pashka, discarding the liquid, and stir in half of the liqueur.
4. Arrange the oranges in a dish and sprinkle them with the remaining liqueur and sugar.
5. Turn the pashka into a small bowl so that it is piled high, above the rim. Chill and serve separately as a 'sauce'.

Beforehand:
Prepare the pashka to the end of step 2 or 3. Slice the oranges, sprinkle with sugar and store in a covered container in the refrigerator.

BUSY COOK'S MENUS

*Denotes that the dish can be prepared in advance to this stage. Any special instructions on storing are given in brackets after this symbol.

Smoked mackerel and cream cheese pâté

—— // ——

Veal chops with marjoram sauce
Small potatoes tossed in herb butter
Green peas

—— // ——

Raspberries in Melba sauce

SMOKED MACKEREL AND CREAM CHEESE PÂTÉ

75 g (3 oz) butter, softened
175 g (6 oz) full-fat soft cheese
350 g (12 oz) smoked mackerel fillets, skinned and flaked
2 teaspoons lemon juice
1 tablespoon chopped chives
freshly ground black pepper
25 g (1 oz) butter
4 small bay leaves, to garnish

Preparation time: 20 minutes

1. Cream together the butter and cheese, stir in the fish, lemon juice, chives and pepper. Beat until the mixture is smooth.
2. Divide the pâté between 4 individual ramekin dishes and smooth the tops. Melt the butter and pour it over the dishes. Tip so that the butter forms a thin, even film. Place a bay leaf to garnish each dish.
3. Cover the dishes with film and store in the refrigerator for up to 2 days.*

RASPBERRIES IN MELBA SAUCE

450 g (1 lb) raspberries, fresh or frozen
Sauce:
350 g (12 oz) raspberries, fresh or frozen
1 teaspoon lemon juice
100 g (4 oz) icing sugar, sifted
To serve:
¼ teaspoon ground cinnamon
25 g (1 oz) icing sugar, sifted
150 ml (5 fl oz) double cream, whipped
1 egg white, stiffly beaten

VEAL CHOPS WITH MARJORAM SAUCE

4 large veal chops
25 g (1 oz) butter
1 tablespoon vegetable oil
1 medium onion, peeled and finely chopped
1 garlic clove, peeled and finely chopped
3 tablespoons chicken stock
3 tablespoons dry vermouth
1 tablespoon chopped marjoram or 1 teaspoon dried marjoram
salt
freshly ground black pepper
4 tablespoons double cream

Preparation time: 10 minutes
Cooking time: 50 minutes

1. Fry the chops in the butter and oil in a flameproof casserole over moderate heat for 4 minutes on each side. Remove the chops and keep them warm.
2. Fry the onion and garlic for 3 minutes, stirring once or twice, then pour on the stock and vermouth and stir well. Return the chops to the dish, add the marjoram, salt and pepper.
3. Bring the sauce to the boil. Cover the dish, lower the heat and simmer for 30 minutes.*
4. Increase the heat, bring the sauce to the boil again and boil to reduce the liquid slightly. Add the cream and allow just to heat through. Taste the sauce and adjust the seasoning if necessary.

Preparation time: 20 minutes, plus thawing time for frozen raspberries

1. Hull fresh raspberries, thaw frozen ones and put them in a serving dish.
2. To make the sauce, hull or thaw the raspberries, sieve them and stir the lemon juice and icing sugar into the purée. Pour over the whole raspberries and stir to mix well. Cover the bowl and chill.*
3. Stir in the cinnamon and icing sugar into the cream and fold in the egg white. Serve separately. This is best made just before serving.

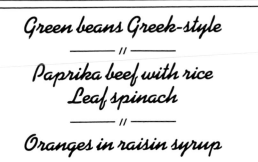

GREEN BEANS GREEK-STYLE

450 g (1 lb) green beans, topped and tailed
100 g (4 oz) button mushrooms, trimmed and sliced
1 lemon, quartered, to serve
Sauce:
1 garlic clove, peeled and finely chopped
1 medium onion, peeled and finely chopped
4 tablespoons olive oil
120 ml (4 fl oz) dry white wine
120 ml (4 fl oz) water
1 tablespoon tomato purée
8 coriander seeds, crushed
a few stalks of savory, if available, or fresh parsley
salt
freshly ground black pepper

Preparation time: 10 minutes
Cooking time: 45 minutes

1. Fry the garlic and onion in the oil over low heat for 10 minutes, stirring frequently. Add the remaining sauce ingredients, adding plenty of pepper, bring to the boil, cover and simmer for 5 minutes.
2. Add the beans and mushrooms, cover and simmer for 25-30 minutes, or until the vegetables are tender, but still crisp. Check the seasoning and adjust, if necessary.
3. Turn the vegetables and sauce into a serving dish and allow to cool. Cover and refrigerate.*
4. Serve cold.

ORANGES IN RAISIN SYRUP

4 tablespoons clear honey
5 tablespoons water
1 tablespoon lemon juice
1 tablespoon dark rum (optional)
6 tablespoons seedless raisins
6 seedless oranges, peeled and thinly sliced
2 tablespoons walnut halves, to decorate

PAPRIKA BEEF WITH RICE

1 medium onion, peeled and thinly sliced
1 garlic clove, peeled and crushed
2 sticks tender celery, thinly sliced
2 tablespoons vegetable oil
50 g (2 oz) butter
450 g (1 lb) minced beef
1 tablespoon plain flour
1 tablespoon paprika
salt
freshly ground black pepper
1 bay leaf
300 ml (½ pint) chicken stock
225 g (8 oz) long-grain rice
100 g (4 oz) button mushrooms, sliced
3 tablespoons soured cream
1 tablespoon chopped fresh parsley, to garnish

Preparation time: 10 minutes
Cooking time: 1 hour 10 minutes

1. Fry the onion, garlic and celery in the oil and half the butter over moderate heat for 4 minutes, stirring once or twice. Add the minced beef and fry for about 8 minutes, stirring to brown it evenly. Stir in the flour and paprika and cook for a further 2 minutes.
2. Add the salt, pepper, bay leaf and stock and bring to the boil. Cover the pan, lower the heat and simmer for about 50 minutes, until the meat is tender.
*(Allow to cool and store in the refrigerator. On the day, reheat and continue with the recipe.)
3. Ten minutes before the meat is cooked, start cooking the rice. Cook it in a large pan of boiling, salted water for 10-12 minutes, until just tender. Drain in a colander and fluff it up with a fork.
4. Fry the mushrooms in the remaining butter for 3-4 minutes over moderate heat.
5. Remove the bay leaf from the meat. Stir in the soured cream and allow just to heat through.
6. Turn the meat on to a heated serving dish and surround it with a ring of rice. Scatter the mushrooms over the meat and garnish with the parsley. Serve with leaf spinach.

Preparation time: 10 minutes
Cooking time: 10 minutes

1. Heat the honey and water, stirring to dissolve the honey. Boil for 2 minutes, then add the lemon juice, rum if used and raisins. Boil for 5 minutes.
2. Pour the hot sauce over the sliced oranges. Leave to cool, then cover and chill.*
3. Decorate with the walnuts to serve.

BUSY COOK'S MENU

Broccoli and yogurt salad

—— // ——

Stir-fried beef
Golden rice

—— // ——

Strawberries in butterscotch sauce

BROCCOLI AND YOGURT SALAD

750 g (1½ lb) broccoli spears, fresh or frozen
salt
150 ml (5 fl oz) plain unsweetened yogurt
1 teaspoon olive oil
1 teaspoon lemon juice
freshly ground black pepper
50 g (2 oz) button mushrooms, thinly sliced
1 tablespoon walnut halves

Preparation time: 10 minutes
Cooking time: 15 minutes

1. Cut fresh broccoli into even-sized pieces, about
2½ cm (1 inch) in length. Cook the fresh or frozen
broccoli in boiling, salted water until it is just tender.
Drain and cool.
2. For the dressing, mix together the yogurt, oil,
lemon juice, salt and pepper. *(Store the cooked
broccoli and the dressing in separate containers in the
refrigerator.)
3. Toss together the broccoli and mushrooms and
pour on the dressing. Toss lightly and garnish with
the walnuts. Serve cold, but preferably not chilled.
The salad improves with being left to stand at room
temperature for at least 20 minutes before serving.

STIR-FRIED BEEF

450 g (1 lb) fillet of beef
2 tablespoons soy sauce
4 teaspoons cornflour
salt
1 garlic clove, peeled and finely chopped
1 cm (½ in) piece fresh ginger, peeled and finely chopped
2 tablespoons vegetable oil
300 ml (½ pint) chicken stock
2 tablespoons dry sherry
6 tablespoons milk
8 spring onions, peeled and thinly sliced
2 spring onions, to garnish
Golden rice:
175-225 g (6-8 oz) rice
1 teaspoon ground turmeric

Preparation time: 10 minutes
Cooking time: 20 minutes, plus marinating

1. Slice the beef very thinly and cut it into 1 cm
(½ inch) wide strips. Mix together 1 tablespoon soy
sauce, 1 teaspoon of the cornflour and a pinch of salt.
Toss the beef in this marinade, cover and leave at
room temperature for about 2 hours, or overnight in
the refrigerator.*
2. Prepare the golden rice. Cook the rice in a pan of
boiling, salted water with the turmeric.
3. Fry the garlic and ginger in the oil over moderately
high heat, stirring, for 1 minute. Add the stock, sherry
and remaining soy sauce, stir and bring to the boil.
Lower the heat and simmer the sauce for 10 minutes.
4. Once cooked, drain the rice and return it to the
pan to keep warm while you finish the stir-frying.
5. Pour the milk on to the remaining cornflour and
stir to make a smooth paste.
6. Increase the heat again, add the beef, any marinade
and the sliced spring onions to the sauce. Stir for
3 minutes. Add the cornflour paste, bring to the boil
and stir for 1-2 minutes, until the sauce thickens.
Taste and add more salt, if necessary. Garnish with
the spring onions. Serve at once, with the golden rice.

STRAWBERRIES IN BUTTERSCOTCH SAUCE

750 g (1½ lb) fresh strawberries, hulled
Sauce:
150 g (5 oz) soft light brown sugar
150 g (5 oz) golden syrup
125 ml (4 fl oz) double cream
3-4 drops vanilla essence

Preparation time: 5 minutes
Cooking time: 10 minutes

1. To make the sauce, heat the sugar and syrup over a
low heat, stirring occasionally, until the sugar has
dissolved. Cook for a further 5 minutes.
2. Remove the pan from the heat and stir in the
cream and vanilla essence. Beat for about 2 minutes,
until the sauce is smooth and glossy. Serve the
strawberries with the sauce hot or cold. *(The sauce
can be made a day ahead, stored in the refrigerator,
and then served cold. It does not reheat well.)

BUSY COOK'S MENU

Melon balls in ginger sauce

— // —

Duckling with honey and grape sauce
Small jacket potatoes
Broccoli spears

— // —

Nutty cream cones

MELON BALLS IN GINGER SAUCE

1 medium cantaloup or honeydew melon
Sauce:
225 ml (8 fl oz) plain unsweetened yogurt
4 teaspoons ginger syrup
4 pieces preserved stem ginger, finely chopped
pinch of grated nutmeg
4 orange slices, to garnish

Preparation time: 20 minutes

1. Halve the melon and scoop out the seeds. Using a vegetable baller or a small teaspoon, scoop the melon flesh into ball shapes and place in a serving dish.
2. Stir together the yogurt, syrup, chopped ginger and nutmeg. Pour the sauce over the melon balls and stir to mix well. Cover the dish and chill in the refrigerator.*
3. Garnish each dish with an orange slice.

DUCKLING WITH HONEY AND GRAPE SAUCE

4 duckling portions, weighing about 400 g (14 oz) each
salt
Sauce:
4 tablespoons clear honey
grated rind and juice of ½ orange
225 g (8 oz) seedless grapes
15 g (½ oz) butter
watercress sprigs, to garnish

Preparation time: 10 minutes
Cooking time: 1 hour 20 minutes
Oven: 180°C, 350°F, Gas Mark 4

1. Prick the duckling pieces all over with a sterilised darning needle or a fork. Rub salt into the skin, so that it crisps well. Place the portions, skin side up, on a rack in a roasting dish.
2. Cook in a preheated oven for about 1¼ hours, or until the meat is tender.
3. Just before the end of the cooking time, heat the honey, orange rind and juice, grapes and butter and bring the sauce to the boil.
4. Transfer the duckling to an ovenproof dish, pour over the sauce and return to the oven for 5 minutes. Serve hot, garnished with the watercress.

NUTTY CREAM CONES

Makes about 12 cones
100 g (4 oz) butter
100 g (4 oz) icing sugar
2 egg whites
4-5 drops vanilla sauce
100 g (4 oz) plain flour, sifted
Filling:
2-3 drops vanilla essence
3 tablespoons blanched almonds, toasted
300 ml (10 fl oz) double cream

Preparation time: 15 minutes
Cooking time: 8 minutes (in 2 batches)
Oven: 220°C, 425°F, Gas Mark 7

1. Beat together the butter and sugar until light and creamy then beat in the egg whites and stir in the vanilla essence. Stir in the flour, a little at a time, until completely incorporated.
2. Grease and flour 2 baking sheets and mark about 6 × 10 cm (4 inch) circles in the flour on each sheet. On one baking sheet, drop the mixture into the marked circles, 2 teaspoons at a time, and spread it evenly to fill the shape.
3. Bake this first batch in a preheated oven for 4 minutes.
4. As soon as you take the biscuits from the oven, lift them one at a time from the baking sheet and shape them quickly into cones. To do this, hold each biscuit in the palm of one hand and with the other wrap 2 sides of the circle to overlap. Stand the cones upright in a dish or casserole until they have cooled.
5. Cook and shape the remaining mixture similarly.
*(The biscuits can be stored in an airtight tin for up to 2 days.)
6. Stir the vanilla essence and most of the almonds into the cream reserving some for decoration. Just before serving, fill the cones with cream and top each one with a toasted almond.

BUSY COOK'S MENU

Curried apple soup

———— // ————

*Wholewheat spaghetti
with tuna fish sauce
Green salad*

———— // ————

Blackcurrant kissel with toasted nuts

CURRIED APPLE SOUP

450 g (1 lb) cooking apples, peeled, cored and chopped
1 medium onion, peeled and sliced
2 sticks tender celery, thinly sliced
40 g (1½ oz) butter, or hard or soft margarine
2 teaspoons curry powder (mild or hot, to taste)
1 tablespoon chopped fresh mint
juice of 1 lemon
600 ml (1 pint) chicken stock
2 tablespoons semolina (wholewheat semolina, if available)
300 ml (10 fl oz) milk or plain unsweetened yogurt
salt
freshly ground black pepper
To garnish:
4 teaspoons sunflower seeds
4 sprigs parsley

Preparation time: 10 minutes
Cooking time: 35 minutes

1. In a large pan, gently fry the apples, onion and
celery in the fat, stirring occasionally, for 5 minutes.
Increase the heat to moderate, stir in the curry
powder and cook for 3 minutes. Add the mint and
lemon juice and pour on the stock, stirring. Bring
slowly to the boil, cover and simmer for 20 minutes,
or until the apples are tender.
2. Liquidize the soup or rub through a nylon sieve.
Put the semolina in the rinsed pan and gradually pour
on the apple purée, stirring all the time. Pour on the
milk or yogurt and bring slowly to simmering point.
Do not allow to boil. Add salt and pepper.*
3. Serve the soup hot, or cold, garnished with the
sunflower seeds and parsley sprigs.

WHOLEWHEAT SPAGHETTI WITH TUNA FISH SAUCE

350 g (12 oz) wholewheat spaghetti
2 teaspoons vegetable oil
50 g (2 oz) butter
1 garlic clove, peeled and finely chopped
2 tablespoons olive oil
200 ml (⅓ pint) chicken stock
3 tablespoons dry sherry
1 × 225 g (8 oz) can tuna fish, drained and flaked
3 tablespoons chopped fresh parsley
freshly ground black pepper
2 tablespoons single cream

Preparation time: 5 minutes
Cooking time: 20 minutes

1. Bring a large pan of water to the boil and add
2 teaspoons salt and the vegetable oil. Cook the
spaghetti for 12-13 minutes, or until it is just tender.
Drain it in a colander and run hot water through it.
Drain again, return to the pan, stir in half the butter
and keep the spaghetti warm.
2. Fry the garlic in the olive oil and remaining butter
over moderate heat for 2 minutes. Pour on the stock
and sherry and boil rapidly for 5 minutes to reduce
the liquid. Stir in the tuna fish and 2 tablespoons of
the parsley. Add salt and pepper, and stir in the
cream. Taste and adjust the seasoning, if necessary.
3. Turn the spaghetti into a heated serving dish, pour
on the sauce and toss lightly. Garnish with the
remaining parsley.

BLACKCURRANT KISSEL

750 g (1½ lb) fresh or frozen blackcurrants
75 g (3 oz) soft light brown sugar
4 tablespoons red wine
juice and grated rind of ½ orange
1 tablespoon arrowroot
2 tablespoons caster sugar
4 tablespoons blanched almonds

Preparation time: 5 minutes
Cooking time: 15 minutes

1. Cook the blackcurrants with the sugar, wine and orange juice and rind over low heat for about 8-10 minutes, or until they are just tender.
2. Stir a little of the juice from the fruit into the arrowroot to make a smooth paste. Stir this into the fruit and simmer gently, stirring all the time, for about 2 minutes, until the mixture thickens.
3. Pour the kissel into a heatproof serving dish and sprinkle with the caster sugar, to prevent a skin forming on top.*
4. Toast the almonds on a baking sheet under a hot grill for about 4 minutes, shaking occasionally to brown them evenly. Arrange the almonds over the pudding in a decorative pattern. Serve warm or cold, with whipped cream and shortbread or sponge finger biscuits. Any leftover kissel makes a delicious sauce with ice cream.

BUSY COOK'S MENU

Fennel and apple salad

———— // ————

Pork fillets in egg and lemon sauce
Small potatoes boiled in their skins
Fresh vegetables

———— // ————

Chocolate pots with cherry brandy

FENNEL AND APPLE SALAD

2 medium-sized roots fennel, trimmed and thinly sliced
2 red-skinned dessert apples, cored and thinly sliced
2 tablespoons seedless raisins, to garnish
Dressing:
150 ml (5 fl oz) soured cream
1 teaspoon cider vinegar
grated rind of ½ orange
1 tablespoon orange juice
pinch of sugar
salt
freshly ground black pepper

Preparation time: 15 minutes

1. To make the dressing, mix together the ingredients. Taste and adjust the seasoning if necessary.
2. Toss together the fennel and apples and immediately toss them in the dressing, so that the apples do not discolour. Garnish the salad with the raisins.

CHOCOLATE POTS WITH CHERRY BRANDY

200 g (7 oz) bitter chocolate
300 ml (10 fl oz) single cream
2 eggs
2 tablespoons cherry brandy
dessert biscuits, such as sponge fingers, to serve

Preparation time: 5 minutes
Cooking time: 5 minutes, plus chilling

PORK FILLET IN EGG AND LEMON SAUCE

2 pork fillets, about 750 g (1½ lb) together
1 tablespoon vegetable oil
50 g (2 oz) butter
100 g (4 oz) button mushrooms, thinly sliced
1 tablespoon chopped fresh parsley, to garnish
Sauce:
25 g (1 oz) butter
2 tablespoons plain flour
300 ml (½ pint) chicken stock
2 eggs
2 tablespoons lemon juice
1 tablespoon water
salt
freshly ground black pepper

Preparation time: 15 minutes
Cooking time: 20 minutes

1. Trim the pork and cut into 2 cm (¾ inch) thick slices.* Fry the meat in the oil and half the butter over moderate heat for about 4 minutes on each side.
2. Add the remaining butter and the mushrooms and cook for 4 minutes, turning the meat once. Remove the meat and mushrooms and keep them warm while you make the sauce.
3. Melt the 25 g/1 oz butter in the pan, stir in the flour and cook for 2 minutes. Gradually pour on the stock, stirring, until the sauce boils.
4. Beat the eggs until they are frothy, beat in the lemon juice and then the water. Reduce the heat to very low.
5. Add about 5 tablespoons of the hot stock to the egg mixture, then pour it into the sauce remaining in the pan. Do not allow the sauce to boil or the egg will scramble. Stir until the sauce thickens, and add salt and pepper.
6. Add the pork and mushrooms to the sauce and serve at once garnished with the parsley.

1. Grate the chocolate or break it into small pieces. Put it into the bowl of an electric blender or food processor.
2. Heat the cream just to boiling point and pour over the chocolate. Blend at high speed for a few seconds until smooth.
3. Break the eggs into the bowl, blend again, add the cherry brandy and blend until the mixture is smooth.
4. Pour into 4 individual serving dishes, cool and then cover and chill overnight in the refrigerator.*
5. Serve with dessert biscuits.

PEARS WITH CAMEMBERT SAUCE

4 ripe dessert pears, peeled, halved and cored
1 tablespoon lemon juice
150 ml (5 fl oz) soured cream
2 tablespoons double cream
50 g (2 oz) Camembert cheese, chopped
pinch of cayenne
sprigs of mint, to garnish

Preparation time: 10 minutes

1. Brush the pears with lemon juice to preserve the colour and arrange them, cut sides up, in a shallow serving dish.
2. Put the soured cream, double cream and Camembert into the bowl of a blender and blend until the mixture is smooth. Sprinkle with cayenne.
3. Pour the sauce over the pears and garnish each one with a sprig of mint.

TURKEY ESCALOPES WITH ANCHOVIES

4 slices turkey breast, about 100 g (4 oz) each
Marinade:
juice of 1 lemon
2 tablespoons vegetable oil
1 teaspoon dried oregano
salt
freshly ground black pepper
2 tablespoons plain flour
75 g (3 oz) fresh breadcrumbs
grated rind of 1 lemon
2 tablespoons chopped fresh mint or parsley
1 egg
1 tablespoon milk
4 tablespoons vegetable oil, for frying
Garnish:
1 × 50 g (2 oz) can anchovy fillets, drained
8 stuffed olives
2 hard-boiled eggs, sliced

Preparation time: 15 minutes
Cooking time: 10 minutes, plus marinating

1. Mix together the lemon juice, oil and oregano for the marinade and add salt and pepper. Pour the marinade into a shallow dish and add the turkey breasts. Cover and leave them to absorb the flavour for 1 hour, or overnight in the refrigerator, turning the meat once.
2. Drain the meat and pat it dry with kitchen paper. Dip the turkey in the flour mixed with salt and pepper until it is well coated.
3. Mix together the breadcrumbs, lemon rind and mint. Beat the egg and milk together and pour on to a plate.
4. Dip the turkey slices into first the egg and then the breadcrumb mixture so that they are well coated.*
5. Fry in the oil for 3-4 minutes on each side, until evenly brown.
6. Arrange the turkey on a heated serving dish. Garnish with the anchovy fillets, each one rolled around an olive, and with the hard-boiled egg slices. Serve hot.

> **Egg marinade**
> Meat, fish or vegetables that are to be coated in breadcrumbs and then deep- or shallow-fried are delicious if you steep them first in the above egg and lemon marinade. It serves a dual purpose – the food not only takes on an extra, subtle flavour but emerges already coated in egg, and just waiting to be tossed in crumbs.
>   Use the marinade for veal, pork, turkey, escalopes, chicken breasts or white fish, and for mushrooms, sliced aubergines and courgettes.

PINEAPPLE RINGS WITH ALMOND MERINGUE

8 slices fresh or canned pineapple about 1 cm (½ inch) thick
25 g (1 oz) butter, melted
2 tablespoons dark rum
Meringue:
2 egg whites
100 g (4 oz) soft light brown sugar
50 g (2 oz) ground almonds

Preparation time: 15 minutes
Cooking time: 10 minutes

1. Drain canned pineapple and pat it dry with kitchen paper. Brush the pineapple on one side with half the butter. Place under a preheated hot grill for 4 minutes. Turn the pineapple, brush with the remaining butter and grill for a further 3-4 minutes, until the fruit is brown and bubbling.
2. While the pineapple is cooking, whisk the egg whites until they are stiff. Fold in half the sugar, whisk again and fold in the remaining sugar and the ground almonds.
3. Sprinkle fruit with the rum.
4. Divide the meringue mixture between the pineapple rings, rough up the top with a fork and grill for 2 minutes, or until the meringue is brown. Serve at once.

Beforehand:
Peel, core and slice fresh pineapple and store it in a lidded box in the refrigerator.

Variation:
For a meringue topping with a hint of the Caribbean, substitute 50 g (2 oz) desiccated coconut for the ground almonds and sprinkle a little extra coconut on top, before grilling. It forms a deliciously crisp, toasty-brown crust that contrasts perfectly with the soft, chewy meringue.

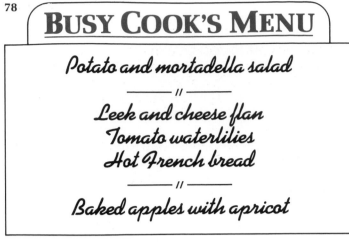

BUSY COOK'S MENU

Potato and mortadella salad

—— // ——

Leek and cheese flan
Tomato waterlilies
Hot French bread

—— // ——

Baked apples with apricot

POTATO AND MORTADELLA SALAD

450 g (1 lb) small potatoes, washed
salt
6-8 spring onions, peeled and thinly sliced
2 tablespoons chopped chives
1 tablespoon chopped chervil or fresh parsley
125 ml (4 fl oz) soured cream
1 tablespoon white wine vinegar
freshly ground black pepper
175 g (6 oz) mortadella sausage, in a piece

Preparation time: 20 minutes
Cooking time: 15 minutes

1. Cook the potatoes in boiling, salted water until
they are just tender. Drain them and, when they are
cool enough to handle, rub off the skins. Slice the
potatoes thickly or cut them in quarters.
2. Stir the onions and herbs into the soured cream,
stir in the vinegar and season well with pepper. Toss
the potatoes in the dressing.
3. Skin the sausage and cut 4 thin slices to garnish.
Cut the remainder into 1 cm (½ inch) cubes. *(Store
the potato salad and mortadella in separate containers
in the refrigerator.)
4. Cut from the edge to the centre of each slice of
mortadella and wrap it into a cone. Just before
serving, stir the diced mortadella carefully into the
potato salad. Turn it into a dish and garnish with the
4 cones.

LEEK AND CHEESE FLAN

225 g (6 oz) plain flour
pinch of salt
175 g (4 oz) hard butter
1 egg yolk
iced water, to mix
Filling:
4 medium leeks, peeled and thinly sliced
salt
15 g (½ oz) butter
1 tablespoon chopped fresh mint
2 eggs
300 ml (10 fl oz) single cream
freshly ground black pepper
100 g (4 oz) Cheddar cheese, grated

Preparation time: 20 minutes, plus chilling
Cooking time: 45 minutes
Oven: 200°C, 400°F, Gas Mark 6;
          190°C, 375°F, Gas Mark 5

To save time, you can use 350 g (12 oz) bought
shortcrust pastry. This, of course, eliminates the
'chilling' time, too.
1. To make the pastry, sift together the flour and salt.
Grate and stir in the butter, then stir in most of the
egg yolk and just enough water to make a firm dough.
Form the dough into a ball, wrap it in film or foil and
chill for 30 minutes.
2. Partly cook the leeks in boiling, salted water for
5 minutes. Drain them and toss them on kitchen
paper. Gently fry them in the butter for 2-3 minutes.
3. Roll out the pastry and line a 23 cm (9 inch) flan
ring on a baking sheet. Trim the edges and prick the
base all over with a fork. Brush the pastry with the
reserved egg yolk. Bake in a preheated oven for
10 minutes, then remove from the oven.*
4. Spread the leeks over the pastry base and sprinkle
on the mint. Beat together the eggs and cream, add
pepper and stir in the cheese.
5. Pour the filling into the pastry case. Reduce the
oven temperature and cook for 25 minutes, until the
filling has set. Serve warm, or cold.
6. Cut the tomato waterlilies by inserting a sharp
knife into a tomato at a right-angle. Work round
making 'V' cuts, and carefully separate the halves.

BAKED APPLES WITH APRICOT

4 medium cooking apples
75 g (3 oz) dried apricots, chopped
75 g (3 oz) soft light brown sugar
a pinch of ground coriander
150 ml (¼ pint) apple juice (the cloudy type is best)
50 g (2 oz) butter or hard margarine

Preparation time: 10 minutes
Cooking time: 40 minutes
Oven: 180°C, 350°F, Gas Mark 4

1. Core the apples and cut a shallow slit around the centre of each one, to prevent the skin from bursting. Arrange the apples in a shallow ovenproof dish.
2. Mix together the apricots, sugar and coriander. Pack the apricot mixture tightly into the apple cavities. Scatter the remaining filling around the apples so that it cooks in the sauce. Pour on the apple juice and dot the apples with pieces of the butter or margarine. *(Loosely cover the apples with foil and store in the refrigerator.)
3. Cook the apples, uncovered, in a preheated oven for about 40 minutes, or until they are just tender. Do not overcook them, or they will collapse and lose their shape. Traditionally, baked apples are served hot, but they are also delicious cold, with whipped cream or ice cream.

INDEX